MW00435763

GUNS
OF THE PEE DEE

TED L. GRAGG

GUNS
OF THE PEE DEE

The Search For The Warship CSS Pee Dee's Cannons

TED L. GRAGG

Published by
Flat River Rock Publishing Division
MBISR, Inc.
Myrtle Beach, South Carolina

Cover/Interior design by Judi Lynn Lake

ISBN 978-0-9794572-3-4
0-9794572-3-8

Printed in the United States of America

myrtle beach • sc

Flat River Rock Publishing Division
MBISR, Inc.
Myrtle Beach, South Carolina
843.293.4344

...they ran the vessel aground; and the prow stuck fast and remained immovable, but the stern began to be broken up....
—Acts 27: 41

For the New South....
Holly, Wendy, John, Shelley, Eddie, & Vaughn

Foreword

Review For *Guns Of The Pee Dee*
Christopher F. Amer
State Underwater Archaeologist
Maritime Research Division
South Carolina Institute of Archaeology & Anthropology
University of South Carolina

Guns of the Peedee is a good read. Author Ted Gragg uses the Confederate Naval shipyard constructed at Mars Bluff on the Great Pee Dee River in South Carolina as a backdrop for a highly readable tale of his and the other members of the C.S.S. Peedee Research and Recovery Team's twenty-year quest to discover the remains of the shipyard. The shipyard was the only Confederate inland naval facility in the state, producing one Macon-class gunboat and several auxillery vessels before being abandoned during the waning years of the conflict.

Mr. Gragg uses historical documents, many of them personal letters including those in Lt. Edward Means' Letterbook (Means was commandant of the shipyard during the last eight months of the conflict), to help him interpret the numerous artifacts and features found at the site and in the river. In so doing he breathes life into the individuals who lived and worked at the shipyard some century and a half ago. There is the first-hand account by one Louise Harllee Pearce, a young lady who travelled with her family in August 1864 to attend the launching of *C.S.S. Peedee*, the only gunboat built at the shipyard. She and her family were caught in one of those deluges that the South is famous for and missed seeing the hull being launched. The discovery of a shoe form led the team to realize that the shipyard had a cobbler and culminated in the chance meeting of that man's great, great grandson last year. The author's attention to detail certainly holds him in good stead. He very logically argues for the Peedee sporting a two-masted rig based on comparison to other gunboats of the Macon class, but also tied to the historically documented installation of large fresh-water tanks designed to extend the seaward range of the gunboat that necessitated the removal of one mast.

Like the two-and-one-half-year tenure of the shipyard, the C.S.S Peedee Research and Recovery Team's quest has been an odyssey. Since its formation in 1995, one member has died, two had heart attacks, many grandchildren were born and two members were married, by Gragg himself. The tangible results of the odyssey include the discovery of two of the three big guns jettisoned from the gunboat Peedee shortly before it was scuttled to avoid capture by General Sherman's advancing troops. Ted and his wife Connie constructed a museum to exhibit and interpret the artifacts and tell the story of the State's only inland Confederate Naval ship-yard and the gunboat that bore the name of the Indian tribe that has inhabited that region of the State since before Europeans explored the region in the 1600s. The quest also produced enduring friendships and forged a professional relationship with the state's Maritime Research Division that has stood the test of time.

This book is a rich tapestry of historical documentation and archaeology filled with Indiana Jones style adventure and suspense (see the artillery shell defusing episode!), sleuthing and personal anecdotes. But most of all it is just a good read. ⸙

...moments of high, proud exultation
that only a discoverer can experience.
—Samuel Eliot Morisison,
Admiral of the Ocean Sea

War Between the States Cannon
What does that mean to the average scuba diver?

With more than three decades of scuba diving, I have recovered many underwater treasures including shipwreck artifacts in the ocean, sharks' teeth in the dark waters of the Cooper River, a Rolex watch from Lake Marion and a tennis bracelet out of Goat Island Landing. There have been search and recoveries of boats, outboard motors, props, guns, anchors, and more from most of the rivers and creeks in the Pee Dee area.

Each time I would find a treasure, it was very exciting and satisfying. But, on September 17, 1995, while diving alone on the Mars Bluff site on the Pee Dee River, I made a find that was more than exciting and satisfying. I found the first of three cannon that history said was on the newly built gunship *CSS Pee Dee*, the nine inch Dahlgren Cannon.

I had never thought that finding one of these guns would be much different than any of my past finds. But nothing can compare! First, was the excitement! I got a strong hit with my White P1000 metal detector and I was digging through eighteen inches of sand to find the smooth muzzle of the nine-inch gun. The feeling that came next was totally unexpected. I was lying on the sandy river bottom holding on to the muzzle so that the current didn't wash me back downstream. I started to relax and realized what had just happened. For 130 years, this gun had been lying here and I was the first person to have had a hand on it since its navy crew threw it overboard. I think this is as close as you can get to the feeling of being on the deck of the *CSS Pee Dee* and helping the crew clear the ship of all the cannon. This is more than exciting.

On September 23, 2006, almost eleven years to the date of the nine inch cannon find, I found the 6.4 inch Brooke Cannon. This was also one of those days that I was in the river alone and my trusty White P1000 metal detector did its job again. Funny, I had been up and down this part of the work site hundreds of times and had missed this Brooke every time. After studying the Brooke's location, I understood why I missed it before. When the Navy crew threw the gun overboard, it landed butt first and was almost standing straight up leaning against a mud bank. To make things worse, it was camouflaged by cut logs that had sunk. These were logs for the sawmill on the shipyard.

This was a moving moment also, but I spent less time contemplating on this dive with the Brooke (I got cold). I guess the satisfaction came later. For days, weeks, and years after the nine inch cannon discovery, I realized that there had been many groups and individuals searching for these cannon for many years and that our group, the CSS Pee Dee Research and Recovery Team went the extra mile! ら

Bob Butler
Diver
C.S.S. Pee Dee Research and Recovery Team

Bob Butler

Prologue

Her broad black face glistened with sweat. Her dark eyes watched me, checking me out, curious-like as she bit deeply into the Moon Pie. The cellophane wrapper surrounding the pie rustled as she shifted it to expose more pie. She paused, averted her gaze, and drank of a bottled Pepsi-Cola.

"Warm, isn't it?" I said.

She nodded and took another bite.

We sat across from each other in the small anteroom of the purchasing agents office. I was hoping to sell electrical equipment to the sewing plant. It was hot in the small room.

I thought of how things had changed in the last eighteen months since I had left the military and returned home with a new wife and a one year old baby girl. I really liked being part of a new family and wished that I were with them at that very moment instead of sitting in a sweltering hot waiting room in the middle of July, 1972. There wasn't even anything lying about to read. Idly I started doodling on my order pad, wondering if there could be anything of interest in Marion, South Carolina instead of just one factory call after another.

The woman's voice startled me. "I sure would likes to be on de river a-fishing right now." She wiped her beaming face with the tail of her overly large red t-shirt and smiled.

She was bored, too, and it really was stifling in the small room. I wasn't alone in wishing I were elsewhere. I smiled back.

"Where do you fish, ma'am?" I asked.

She grinned again, her teeth flashing whitely against the dark hued skin. "On the Pee Dee, the Great Pee Dee River. Over near the old roadway bridge. I wish that I was sitting on that old iron log right now. Bound to be cooler! Phew, it is hot in this room!"

An iron log? My thoughts of home suddenly evaporated. Iron log? I had heard of the missing cannon from the Confederate warship Peedee since Dr. Frank Sanders, a local optometrist, had spun tales of local historical lore to keep an eight year old boy from being worried and bored in his Conway office.

"Ma'am. You mentioned an iron log. Is it nearby?" I waited eagerly for her answer.

"Matter of factly, that ol' log's not far from where we is now. Big ol' heavy thing, that log. Just juts out from the riverbank when the water's real low-like. It's perfect, cause the catfish lurk around it then and some of them are real big, like this"...and she stretched out her arms to illustrate the size of the fish.

Her answer was fantastic. She really could be sitting on a cannon barrel.

I began another question. "Ma'am, does the..."

Before I could finish the query, a bell rang in the adjoining room. She left to continue her work shift as a sewing machine operator. Suddenly the small hot room seemed rather large as I envisioned a riverbank scene scattered with wreckage from a missing Southern warship. I would have almost followed her through the workroom door still asking questions if the call from the purchasing agent's receptionist had not brought me back to reality. Little did the friendly machine operator know that her concise sentences would initiate an interest and a search that would span the next four decades of my life and that of my family, create a renewed interest in the history of the area by the State of South Carolina, and result in the recovery of historical artifacts and armaments that had been lost for one hundred and fifty years. The quest had begun. ƻ

Chapter 1

THE ONSET OF THE War for Southern Independence, or as some call it, the American Civil War, in 1860 saw tremendous changes in naval warfare. The newly formed Naval Department of the Confederate States of America was quick to recognize, adopt, and utilize the advantages of ironclad warships, heavier armament and ordnance, and modern naval tactics. The days of wooden ships, close-in broadside engagements, and sail were nearing their end.

The war effort by the United States Navy included the 'Anaconda Plan' devised by the United States Army General-in-Chief Winfield Scott wherein a blockading fleet would encompass the coastlines of the seceding states of the Confederacy thus prohibiting resupply, the putting of new ships to sea, and the importation of foodstuffs and weapons. In the process of doing this, existing vessels and naval facilities of the newer Confederate nation were being captured or overrun by the Union forces. Meanwhile Union forces could advance down the Mississippi River to cut the South in half, invade the Tennessee River Valley, invade Georgia, and lastly capture Richmond, Virginia. The strangulation of the South would be similar to the wrapping of the region in the coils of a gigantic serpent, therein the name Anaconda Plan.

One of the most revered officers in Confederate naval service, Matthew Fontaine Maury, suggested the building of a large force of small wooden gunboats to be utilized in the defense of the Confederacy's rivers and smaller ports. These vessels, known as the Hampton Class of Maury gunboats, were to be 112 feet in length, 21 feet in beam, and draw only 6 feet of water. The Confederate Congress seized upon this idea and authorized its funding with two million dollars. Confederate States Naval Secretary Stephen R. Mallory proposed a plan for a fleet of wooden vessels as well and issued orders for Naval Constructor John L. Porter to draw up plans for these new vessels. Porter lengthened Maury's design and widened the beam, creating the Macon Class of vessel. The Naval Department then issued orders to construct new naval yards and shipbuilding centers along the nation's inland waterways to prevent new ships being built from attacks by the United States Navy. A number of these new wooden-hull gunboats were approved for construction in the fall of 1861 by Secretary Mallory. The new shipyards commissioned to build these vessels were Pensacola, Florida; Jacksonville, Florida; Elizabeth City, North Carolina; Mars Bluff, South Carolina; Savannah, Georgia; Washington, North Carolina; and Mobile, Alabama. Four of these vessels would be completed and commissioned, the *CSS Peedee* from Mars Bluff, South Carolina; the *CSS Chattahoochee* in Saffold County, Georgia; the *CSS Morgan* and the *CSS Gaines* of Mobile, Alabama. Other new inland yards were opened at Edwards Ferry, North Carolina; Saffold, Georgia; Memphis, Tennessee; and Columbus, Georgia. All were engaged in the effort to construct a new and powerful navy.[1] ⟩

---

[1]William N. Still Jr., <u>Confederate Shipbuilding,</u> (University of Georgia Press, Athens, GA) 13, 33

Chapter 2

IT WAS LATE FALL, 1862. Lt. Alphonse Barbot, CSN, leaned against the rail of the newly constructed world-renown drawbridge that spanned the waters of the Great Pee Dee River between the towns of Marion Courthouse and Florence, South Carolina. He was under orders from Flag Officer D. N. Ingraham, commander of the Charleston, South Carolina naval office to locate, inspect, and investigate likely spots along the navigable inland rivers of South Carolina for a likely site of a new naval yard. He gazed upstream toward the site that he had chosen for the construction of the Confederate Naval Yard at Mars Bluff.[2]

Barbot was comfortable with his choice. The new drawbridge offered easy travel between the coastal counties to the Southeast and the inland westward regions. Rail connection throughout the Confederacy to the Mississippi River was provided by the nearby Wilmington, Weldon, and Manchester Railroad that crossed upstream on a modern swing bridge. A convenient narrow gauge spur line ran from the main tracks alongside the Mossy Point road toward a new warehouse that nestled close to the river.[3] Easy river traffic access was afforded by the ferry slip that nestled just below the bridges. A small logging operation was active on the chosen

[2] Leah Townsend, *"The Confederate Gunboat Pedee",* (The South Carolina Historica Magazine, Vol. LX, No. 2, April 1959) 66
[3] Lawrence E. Babits, Lynn Harris, Nolen Caudell, and Adam Edmonds, "Prehistoric Pottery, Munitions and Caulking Tools: Archaeological And Historical Investigations at Mars Bluff Confederate on the Great Pee Dee River" (Program in Maritime Studies Summer Field School 2009, East Carolina University-2010)

site. The nearby plantations offered a ready source of foodstuffs for the workmen employed by the new yard. This indeed was a choice location for the new naval yard. Satisfied, Barbot returned to the Charleston Naval office and submitted his report and suggestions to Flag Officer Ingraham.

Some months passed and on March 16, 1863, a formal land rental agreement was reached by the Confederate Navy and the current landowner, Mr. Joseph Bird. This lease agreement was signed by 1st. Lt. William M. Dozier, CSN, Captain S. Thomson, and Joseph Bird. The lease stated that the Confederate States Department of the Navy would rent a ten-acre tract known as "Bird's Landing" for the sum of $200.00 dollars per year. The lease stipulated that the property's trees could be used, buildings could be erected, and that the sole purpose of the lease was the building of gunboats.[4]

Lt. Dozier was following the orders given to him by Secretary of the Navy Mallory in a letter dated December 16, 1862:

> "Sir: The Department relies upon you to complete the gunboat from the construction of which you are ordered, in the shortest possible time." [5]

Once the lease for the Naval Yard had been signed and back-dated to cover the work underway on the site since January 1, 1863, Dozier relinquished oversight of the construction of the first vessel, the gunboat *CSS Peedee*, to Lt. Van R. Morgan, CSN. Morgan immediately moved the command center to the Confederate States Naval Station at Marion Courthouse, South Carolina. From there he traveled daily by either buggy or train to the naval yard to oversee the continued construction of both the vessel and the naval yard. In May of 1863 he wrote a friendly letter to Catesby ap Roger Jones congratulating him on his April 29, 1863 promotion to

---

[4] Marion County Deed Book "Z", 1863, Marion County Courthouse, Marion, SC, 417-418.
[5] Op. cit., Townsend, 66.

Commander, Confederate States Navy (CSN). Jones, who had been the Executive Officer aboard the Confederate States Ship *Virginia (Merrimac)* at the battle of Hampton Roads, was by this time commanding the *CSS Chattahoochee* at Columbus, Georgia. In his letter, Lt. Morgan asks for the shipment of 4 each three fold blocks (a block is a nautical term for a three groove pulley as part of a block and tackle) and advises Jones that the ship he is building is 150 feet in length, drawing 7½ feet of water (the draught of the vessel), and that he is depending on a centerboard (an adjustable keel that drops through a slot in the center of the hull of a ship or boat to provide ballast and stability) to support the vessel on the high sea while carrying four guns.[6] This is an exceedingly important statement in the history of the Mars Bluff Naval Yard and the *CSS Peedee*. This statement is the confirmation of the intent of Secretary of the Navy Mallory that the *CSS Peedee* would be one of several new vessels constructed to follow in the wake of the success of the high seas raider *CSS Alabama.* ❧

---

[6] Lt. Van R. Morgan, Personal letter to Lt. Commander Jones, CSN, May 1863, Library of Congress Area 8 file, 838-841, Library of Congress, Washington, D.C.

Chapter 3

BY EARLY 1863, THE Confederate States Naval Yard at the former Bird's Landing on the Great Pee Dee River, now and forever known as Mars Bluff Naval Yard, had really expanded. Vigorous activity was occurring throughout the yard and the sounds of hammers and mallets, the cries of workmen as they advanced their labors, and the screech of saws against hard pine and oak rent the air. New buildings abounded. A waterwheel provided power to a series of belts and pulleys that drove saws and other machinery in various buildings along the bluffs above the Great Pee Dee River. A cobbler's shed, two small forges, two sawmills, a cooper's shed, a planning mill, a barracks, a headquarters building or office, a main pier that jutted over 60 feet out into midstream and ran north 190 feet parallel to the bank below the naval yard, a vessel launching ramp, a stone, brick, and masonry breakwater, and an extended causeway from the ferry slip to the yard's pier, a telegraph station, a turning lathe and machine shop, and a brick and masonry chimney and boiler were built and in use at the naval yard by mid 1864.

The original mission of the Mars Bluff Naval Yard was to build vessels of war. But as the war progressed the naval yard grew in size and scope. Its operations became vital to the Confederate ports of Charleston and Wilmington in that it became a transfer point for supplies shipping from the Confederate arsenals and manufacturing sites of Selma, Alabama; Charlotte, N.C.; Petersburg, Va.; and Richmond, Virginia via the Wilmington,

Weldon, and Manchester Railroad.[7, 8, 9] These transfers from Mars Bluff were accomplished by mule and wagon as well as teams of oxen along the region's roads, by rail, or by two river steamers, the Dixie and the Ripley, with the latter being built at the Mars Bluff Naval Yard.[10,11,12]

Following the defeat of the armed forces of the Confederate States of America, the United States Navy sent a boat crew under the command of Ensign Sturgis Center to inventory the remains of the Mars Bluff Naval Yard. His detailed listing of the items left behind following the Confederate navy's retreat from the yard give an overview of the quantity of material and supplies stored at the yard during the major war effort. Center lists the following: Green or uncured pine, oak, and ash lumber, 2000 pounds of ½" round iron bar stock for bolts, 2000 pounds of ⅜" round iron stock, 1800 pounds of ⅜" square iron, 300 feet of 1½" round iron, 3 steam engines, one donkey engine, 1200 feet of anchor chain, 3", 4", 6.4", 7", and 9" ordinance and munitions for same, powder, grape shot, canister, two howitzers, two naval steam engines sized for torpedo boats, extra sail material, 5643 pounds of copper and brass as well as the machinery and tools from the naval yard that were on the deck of the abandoned 128 foot tender built for the living quarters of the crew of the Confederate cruiser, the *CSS Peedee*.[13]

This impressive list of materiels of war remaining at the Mars Bluff Naval Yard following the cessation of hostilities illustrates the effective concentration, storage, and transferring of supplies to other naval commands.

---

[7] Lt. Edward Means, Lt. Edward Means Order Book, (LSU Library Collection, Baton Rouge, La.) 4-6
[8] Op.cit., Still, Jr., 31
[9] Larry J. Daniel and Riley W. Gunter, Confederate Cannon Foundaries, (Pioneer Press, Union City, TN. 1977) 74-81.
[10] Maxwell Clayton Orvin, In South Carolina Waters, 1861-1865 (Nelson's Southern Printing and Publishing Co., Charleston, SC)
[11] Op. cit., Means, 31
[12] W. F. Clayton, The Confederate States Navy, (Harrel's Printing House, Weldon, NC.1910), 105.
[13] Acting Ensign Sturgis Center, USN., Report to Lt. Commander R.L. Law, USN., Port Royal, S.C. 10-20-1865

Provisions and food sources for the personnel employed at the naval yard were acquired from the surrounding area, the Waccamaw Neck, and Georgetown, South Carolina. The provisions consisted of molasses, rice, beans, corn, ham, fish, flour, beef, and syrup. An outbreak of hog cholera in 1863 destroyed the local livestock and supplies of meat had to be procured from Charlotte, N.C. The destruction of 5000 bushels of rice in the Waccamaw Neck above Georgetown during an upriver raid by the United States Navy vessel *U.S.S. Cimmarron* caused concern among the officers at the naval yard. But even with this event, there were ample foodstuffs available within the region to feed the yard's personnel.[14, 15]

The growing importance of the Mars Bluff Naval Yard and its command headquarters at Marion Courthouse, S.C., created an awareness among the state leadership of South Carolina and the military commands in Charleston, S.C. and Richmond, Virginia, of the need for a viable defense of the yard from a possible Yankee invasion.

Fort Finger, a small fortified battery on a high bluff above the Great Pee Dee River was built to protect the naval yard, the railroad bridge, and the vital river waterway. This battery was constructed on the west bank of the river some few miles below the Mars Bluff Ferry. Other fortifications, unmanned, were constructed at various areas along the river's course as it meandered the one hundred miles or so to Winyah Bay and the Atlantic Ocean. These fortifications were part of an arrangement of defense provided for by an act of the state government and paid for with funds provided by the South Carolina Executive Council. These battery sites along the Great Pee Dee River would be manned and armed by contingencies of Charleston based flying coastal artillery should an invasion

---

[14] Naval History Division, Naval Historical Center, <u>Civil War Naval Chronology</u>, 1861-1865, (Washington, D.C.) IV, 47
[15] Op. cit., *Means*, 45.46

occur. Sunken stone rafts as well as log barriers with chains connecting across the navigable channel of the river were included in these defensive postures. Further, a regular guard detail of Confederate infantry was assigned permanent guard duty and stationed at the Mars Bluff Naval Yard following continued problems with escaped Union Army prisoners from the Confederate stockade in nearby Florence, S.C.[16]

Work progressed rapidly on the five vessels under construction at the naval yard. The site became a very effective and productive undertaking for the Confederate States of America. There was little chance of molestation or interest from the United States military forces until the invading northern forces under the command of General William Tecumseh Sherman penetrated the area in early 1865. ⌇

---

[16] Charles E. Cauthen, editor, <u>Journals of the South Carolina Executive Councils of 1861-1862</u>, (South Caroling Archives Department, Columbia, SC., 1956) 94, 111, 115, 156, 187, 188

Chapter 4

THE DAY WAS HOT, stifling hot, and muggy, that kind of hot that just descends from above and surrounds one with the thickness of the heat. The air was full of the decaying odor of the river swamp. Myriads of mosquitoes buzzed around us in hordes; busying themselves with harassing and stinging assaults on us as we cut our way with machetes through the dense undergrowth bordering the river's edge. Our goal was to advance from the railroad trestle along the water's edge of the Great Pee Dee River until we reached an area of high bluffs a mile or so upriver. A drenching Carolina low-country rain storm had just passed, creating additional oozing of the river mud and decaying matter that covered the low lying area that we were attempting to cross. Each yard that we advanced required the hacking away with the machetes at the tangled brush and intertwined vines and limbs that created a barrier toward further penetration of the Carolina low country jungle. The mud sucked at our feet. We were dripping in sweat. The day was heating up and the occasional sighting of a slithering water moccasin didn't make matters easier.

I looked back at Holly, my eldest daughter. She had been just a baby when my search for the Mars Bluff Naval Yard had begun. Now, here it was, July 4, 1994, and still, there was no tangible evidence of the existence of the Confederate war effort in this area. Innumerous attempts along the Great Pee Dee River from the old and decaying remains of the wooden bridge spanning the muddy brown waters between the community of Peedee and the city of Florence, South Carolina, to the high bluffs at the power line crossing upriver had not yielded any definitive results. Like all treasure hunters, I continued to search the area, hoping for that one tangible find that would lead to a resolution of the mystery surrounding the ghostly and elusive Confederate Cruiser *Peedee* and the vindication of the years of searching. Time continued to pass. Wendy, my younger daughter accompanied me on the searches while her older sister began college. Our family life went on, but the nagging mystery continued to haunt me. Just one more expedition, one more time, X marks the spot, don't you know! The *Peedee*, the Naval Yard, it's still out there, calling, beckoning. Just one more time. Now, my girls were grown and in college. I promised myself and Connie my ever patient wife that, if nothing were found, this would be the last foray, the last of my searching for the elusive Confederate Naval Yard.

I would have been more discouraged then had I known of the other searchers that had failed to locate the missing guns of the Confederate warship and the naval yard. The list now seems endless, beginning with the efforts of the U.S. Navy in the first year following the war, 1866. Then came the U.S. Army's Corps of Engineers at the turn of the 20th century followed by the United Daughters of the Confederacy in 1925. These valiant ladies initiated a program to remove the brass propellers from the exposed remains of the destroyed *CSS Peedee* and mount them at the Florence Library in downtown Florence, S.C., as a lasting memorial to the Confederate soldiers and sailors of the region. They in turn were followed by a group of local businessmen in 1954 led by Mr. Frank Martin of Florence and Mr. E.C. Godfrey of Darlington. They wanted to salvage the wreck of the *CSS Peedee*, locate the missing cannon, and create a tourist attraction on the Florence side of the Great Pee Dee River alongside Highway 76. This group managed with the use of log skidders to remove some 36 feet or so from the wreckage of the old warship and drag it into position alongside the highway.

Unfortunately, the skidders changed the texture of the river's bottom and possibly scattered more evidence and artifacts of the ship's demise and history than were located. The enterprise failed in finding any cannon or machinary other than the ship's boiler.

After some years of misuse and decay, Mr. Alan Schafer of Dillon, South Carolina purchased the remains of their salvage with a view of building another attraction, "Conferderate Land" near the present site of South of the Border. This project was abandoned and the salvaged portion of the shipwreck was buried as fill during the construction of Interstate I-95. Later, in the early 1970s, the Honorable E. N. Ziegler pursuaded the U.S. Navy to send a team of divers into the river in search of the canon near the site where the earlier salvage operation had occurred. They were equipped with the latest remote sensing devices to aid their search. It was futile as well.

In the next few years, other interested area and national historians began to submit information requests concerning the naval yard and the warship to the University of South Carolina's Institute of Archaeology and Anthropology. Dr. Robert Stephenson, Director of the Institute at that time forwarded the requests to Mr. Alan B. Albright, the Institute's Underwater Archaeologist.

At the same time, Mr. Albright received a letter from a renowned author expressing interest in locating the legendary site. Private funding was provided for a project through South Carolina Underwater Archaeological Research Council, Inc., for an abbreviated study of the Mars Bluff site and an on-site evaluation due to the possible finding of the remains of the torpedo boat built at the Confederate Naval Yard. Again, the evaluation and search yielded no tangible results.[17] Years passed. The South

---

[17] Michael O. Hartley, "The Mars Bluff Naval Yard, An Archeoligical Evaluation", (South Carolina Institute of Anthropology And Archaeology, 1983)

Carolina Institute of Archaeology and Anthropology still had an interest in the area, but funding wasn't readily available to further pursue this endeavor.

Meanwhile, Mr. Christopher F. Amer joined the staff of the Institute in 1987 and became the South Carolina State Underwater Archaeologist and the Head of the Maritime Research Division. He was instrumental in the creation and passage of the S.C. Underwater Antiquities Act of 1991 that protected artifacts in state waters. Two other men, Bob Butler and Ronnie Sommersett, hobby divers, were searching vigorously on the Florence side of the river for any remains from the wrecked warship. Neither Chris, Bob, or I knew one another in the summer of 1994, but events were about to transpire that would unite us in lasting friendships.

True to the past, as in all of the attempts mentioned before and my searches in the past, it was almost noon and nothing had been seen or found that was indicative of the Civil War period. Our metal detectors hadn't emitted a single promising beep and the heat was becoming more oppressive. We had traveled about 500 yards upstream from the trestle. I was preparing to call the day a loss when I noticed an interesting wooden plank jutting from a mud-covered pile of debris.

The pile was just the perfect sitting height for me. I was cross, aggravated at our failure again, hot, and just plain disgusted. I sat down on the edge of the debris pile and begin poking idly with my machete at the pointed wooden plank that protruded from the mound of dirt. My daughter Holly took an interest in what I was doing and joined me in the effort by clearing debris away from the plank with her shovel.

Soon, Perry Doan, a friend who had accompanied us joined in the effort as more planking became exposed. It wasn't long before we had uncovered the remains of a 15 foot skiff. Interestingly, the top side and bottom of the old hull was covered in thick pine tar or pitch. Several inches of the gunnel were still attached to the left or port side of the hull. All of the exposed nails were iron and appeared to be blacksmith made. It was a fascinating find and definitively dated the search area in the mid to late 19th century.

Longboat Hull

Perry roused himself from the pile of debris and walked 12 feet or so to the river's edge and knelt to wash the mud from his hands. He yelled, loudly, when he placed his hands in the water. Holly and I rushed to his side fearing that he had been struck by one of the ever-present cottonmouth serpents. Just as we came close, he lifted a nine-inch cannonball from the water. The fuse was missing and the brass from the fuse socket gleamed bright yellow in the sunlight. There it was. Pure and simple. Proof at last. The Naval Yard had existed, it was here, or at least nearby.

I knelt at the water's edge and moved my hands around in the water as well and uncovered a 4" stand of canister, the favored round of Civil War cannoneers against enemy troops and ship's rigging. And then Holly found more canister parts, balls, hinged handle tops and bottom plates. We exhausted that treasure trove of relics and moved slowly upriver, metal detecting along the bank and water's edge. More ordnance from the period came to light as well as a couple of axe blades.

Cannister Plates and Sabot

Stand of Cannister

This time we wouldn't go home empty handed. This was the beginning of a twenty year odyssey that would see the formation of the CSS Peedee Research and Recovery Team, the conducting of two intensive surveys for the State of South Carolina, the location of the missing cannon from the *CSS Peedee,* the land location and marking of the Confederate Naval Yard, and the founding of the South Carolina Civil War Museum. Along the way two divers suffered heart attacks and survived, we experienced two marriages within the team, the unexpected demise of William Keeling, our on-site archeologist, and witnessed the advent of five grandchildren without deviating from the mission of proving the existence of the Confederate war effort on the banks of the Great Pee Dee River.

That July 4 day of 1994 we harvested artifacts along the river's edge until exhaustion overtook us. We hiked out and moved my Ford pickup around closer to the bluffs where we could load the proof without having to drag the artifacts 500 yards through the river swamp. Our arrival home that day was tumultuous, to say the least. The next day we began sorting through the artifacts, cleaning them and preparing them for preservation, and creating a journal of the discovery and finds. Perry Doan was the only one among us certified as a scuba diver. We enlisted the aid of Captain James "Crunch" Wasson of Myrtle Beach and planned the next foray into the Confederate stronghold. The second trip a week later yielded as much information and artifacts as the prior excursion. We met Mr. Wiles Clemmons on the second trip and asked his permission to work from his property that bordered the river as he had a private boat ramp. He agreed and for the next three months we worked the site alone, learning step by step the rudiments of underwater and riverine archaeology.

Chapter 5

ONE EVENING NOT LONG into October, I received a visit from Bob Butler and Ronnie Sommersett. Ronnie and I had known one another for years because of our mutual shooting interests and competitive shooting meets that we had attended, but Bob and I had never met.

Bob began the conversation. "I heard that you had located some interesting artifacts from the old Confederate Naval Yard."

I looked at him, puzzled. "Where did you hear that?" I began a verbal sparring match.

"I'd like to see them." He said.

I looked across the room at Ronnie. By that time my wife had entered the room. Her comment went something like, "Hi, Ronnie. Who is this with you?"

Bob spoke again. "My name's Butler, Bob Butler. I've been looking for the warship *CSS Peedee* or the Naval Yard. What did you find?"

I glanced at Connie and she shrugged her shoulders.

Ronnie spoke up then. "He's alright, Ted. He's not going to raid your site. We both dive together, so relax."

We did just that and began to share experiences. Bob and Ronnie had found a few items on the west side of the river, one of them a carriage bearing from a Naval 24 Pounder gun carriage. Our group had found several also on the eastern shore; and not knowing what they were, sent one of them to the curator of the

West Point Museum at the United States Army Academy to see if they could identify the item. The bearing and their response were returned almost immediately with an identification of the item. Therefore, I was able to tell Bob and Ronnie what they had found.

Together, the four of us decided that evening to combine our efforts and work together as a team. We needed the black water diving experience and equipment that these men possessed and they in turn wanted to be included in our find. It was the perfect arrangement, so together we formed the CSS Peedee Research and Recovery Team.

The next two weeks saw major changes in the exploratory expeditions in our seeking of knowledge about the Confederate States Navy Yard at Mars Bluff. Bob was willing to serve as the dive master on all the underwater exploration efforts and I would supervise the land efforts and handle the press and media exchanges. We would jointly share the direction of the team's efforts. This became an excellent example of a partnership and to this day there has never been a need to change it or a problem that we couldn't solve.

The next dive occurred two weeks later. That dive brought some extremely interesting artifacts to the surface. Earlier, the first team had located what appeared to be some of the items from the ship's carpenter's locker...three perfect carpenter's squares that were so well preserved that once cleaned and stabilized, the inch markings could be utilized as well as those on a modern square...even down to the importation mark of "MADE IN ENGLAND". No doubt of the time period for those items! Imagine, those squares had been transported through the Yankee blockade into the Southern Confederacy and distributed into the military supply system. Other tool items appeared like chisels still in their original green paint with the tool maker's marking from Providence, Rhode Island (contraband perhaps), hammers, a caliper, hand drill bits, screwdrivers, and window sash hooks and pulleys. This was a puzzle because we all knew that the ship had been blown up down river. Why were these items lying here on the bottom of the river, covered in mud and cut logs? Another puzzle began.

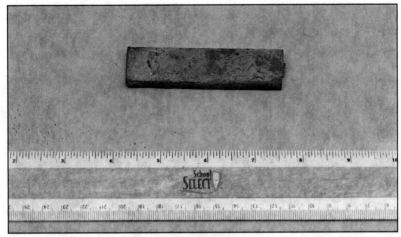

Inspectors Stamp

Inspectors Stamp with V

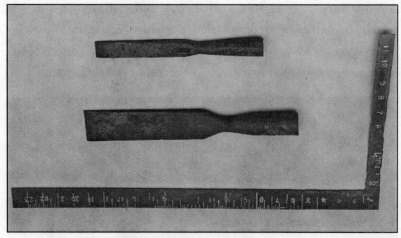

Top: Wood Chisels and Carpenter's Square
Bottom: Ax Head and a flat bastard file

A week later, part of the answer to that puzzle appeared from the murky depths of the river. The water flow in the Great Pee Dee River is affected by the damming of the river in North Carolina. This sometimes causes controversy between North and South Carolina in time of drought as the river is undammed in South Carolina and the need for hydroelectric power in North Carolina can restrict needed water in the riverbed. Once weekly though, on Tuesday, the water level drops in the Great Pee Dee River and

24 pounder cannon naval carriage wheel axle bearing.

this oft times exposes log jams and sandbars that tantalizingly hide major artifacts.

As a team, we had, knowing the change in current and water flow, decided to begin investigating the site on Tuesdays at low water as well as on the weekend. So this time, on Tuesday, much to our surprise, the lower remnants of an old pier began to appear above the surface of the water. Just inches of wooden pilings appeared at first, then gradually a foot or more jutted above the surface of the water. Our three divers began an organized exploratory search around the pilings. Remarkably, they discovered that beneath the surface, the original pier extended out from the eastern riverbank 75 feet or so and then turned upstream at a 30 degree angle using the shoreline as a baseline. The old pier stretched for almost 190 feet along the shoreline.

This answered the question about the possibility of a ship carpenter's toolbox. It probably wasn't a tool box, but instead the shipwright's locker itself from the vessel. We suspected that the ship had been moored at the dock following its one up-river wartime mission. Then, upon orders to scuttle the vessel, all of the equipment aboard her was thrown overboard. This was supposition, but it later turned out to be a proven fact. And, sure enough, as the day wore on another accumulation of ship's artifacts was found not far from the position of the earlier finding of the tools. By this time, we had learned a few simple archaeological rules on our own. We were making charts, maps, and listing the location and depths of the items we recovered from the dark water. These finds and the ones that followed were clearly charted against a fixed baseline with compass coordinates. These new finds or recovered artifacts included sail rings, cleats, a couple of rope or iron hawser guides, and most remarkable, the remains of a wooden block and tackle set, and a cargo hook. This site was appearing to be strewn with artifacts of a nautical setting. We still found the occasional trace of modern civilization intermingled with the 19th century artifacts...pop bottles, whiskey bottles, a broken bathroom sink, parts of an outboard motor, etc.

But, it was time to get really serious about the whole affair and contact the state. This site appeared to be too large and historically important to ignore. We decided at that point to contact the Institute of Archaeology and Anthropology. I arranged an appointment with the South Carolina State Underwater Archaeologist, Chris Amer. Several of us from the team journeyed to Columbia to meet him. We carried several artifacts to show him and requested a serious site inspection. Chris was very helpful. He expressed an interest in the work that we had done and thanked us for coming to him with the find. He told us of the new law that had been passed some months before and suggested that we apply for an Intensive Survey License from the state. There were many requirements for completion of an intensive survey application. We were advised that of course, we could continue as hobby divers and report all findings to the Institute, but if we were really serious, well....

We called a meeting of our group upon our return and discussed the terms of application for the Intensive Survey. Should we locate the cannon, this survey would be a pre-requisite for applying for a salvage permit.

South Carolina was then and is now one of the very few states that employs a state Underwater Archaeologist and maintains a viable, active, and on-going Underwater Archaeology effort that is fully funded and provisioned by the state. This effort is recognized throughout the United States as being one of the foremost and advanced efforts toward conservation of a valuable underwater cultural resource. Due to this, the South Carolina legislature created and passed the Underwater Antiquities Act of 1976 to protect the antiquities that rested in the abundant waters of the state. The South Carolina Institute of Archaeology and Anthropology (SCIAA) was charged with the oversight of this new law as well as bearing the responsibility of maintaining a database of underwater archaeology sites and conducting underwater site studies determined to be in the best interests of the people of South Carolina. This act was further modified and improved with the passage of an updated act in 1991. Our team, the CSS Peedee Research and Recovery Team would become the first group under the new law to be issued an Intensive Survey License. So we, and members of SCIAA, were going to learn together. In all fairness, the situation created the best of both worlds for us because being the spearhead group, we probably received more allocated time and training than would normally have been expected. It paid off for us and the state as the years progressed as we were able to set baselines, record items sampled during the survey, and prepare ways of artifact preservation for exhibition due to the intensive training given our team by SCIAA. Not only did all of our team benefit from the training and guidance, but very strong friendships began and have endured throughout the project and so still exist today.

One of the requirements for the Intensive Survey permit was that the majority of our team members or at least those involved in the underwater exploratory efforts had to attend the University sponsored underwater archaeologist training at the Charleston, South Carolina field office of SCIAA. This program was developed by Dr. Lynn Harris as a means to offer an educational program consisting of organized courses and workshops in underwater archaeology and artifact conservation. This program along with a vocational underwater archaeology manual that she formulated served as an informative tool to acquaint the public with the opportunities and ongoing studies conducted by SCIAA. This would require several days away from our jobs and businesses. We all concurred that it was necessary, so the next week Director Chris Amer was notified of our decision and arrangements were made for enrollment in the next course.

In the meantime, we were to be allowed to continue the operation as hobbyists. A public hearing had to be scheduled for our presentation of our plans and goals for the site along with any possible environmental impacts. We would need the oversight services of a qualified archaeologist to supervise our field activities and oversee conservation of the sampled artifacts. Each member of our team and staff had to submit a full financial statement and an indication of the ability to financially support the on-going work at the site during the time period of the Intensive Survey Permit. Each member was required to submit a resume listing his or her experience, education, and training in the maritime archaeology field or a related source of study. A list of equipment to be used by the team was required as well as a detailed synopsis of excavation, recovery, conservation, and stabilization of all artifacts.

An in-depth research plan of the site was requested and if possible to include any adjacent land sites that could offer information as to the formation and operation of the naval yard area. The application required the arranging for a surface and underwater site survey by the South Carolina Institute of Archaeology and Anthropology's archaeologists and divers. Should their findings concur with ours that the site indeed had historical merit, and that we had completed the other requirements as well as providing information on artifact preservation and maintenance; and that there was no negative public or environmental impacts created by our work, then a permit could possibly be granted to allow us to continue our work with supervision by the state of South Carolina.

Furthermore, each day's work on site had to be documented with a listing of each item recovered from the river, the labeling of each item, and its placement by numbered location on a map grid based upon a common 'baseline'. Weekly reports had to be made by the divers indicating time exposure in the water, mean temperatures, and water conditions along with a report of all items encountered or recovered for the survey.

Boy howdy, we were learning a lot about underwater archaeology. There was more to being Indiana Jones than just dashing off madly into the wilderness. ⟫

Chapter 6

"ONE SEAGOING STEAM GUNBOAT of 5 guns is advancing to completion, machinery ready."[18] (Great Pee Dee River, S.C., about August 30, 1863.) This statement was part of a report sent to Secretary of the Navy Mallory in 1863. Later, Confederate States Secretary of the Navy Stephen Mallory in a report dated April 30, 1864, referred to the "steam gunboat *Pedee* commanded by Lt. O. F. Johnston as being in commission".[19]

Mars Bluff, near the Naval Yard of the Great Pee Dee River, above the ferry...early in 1864,... on a sunlit morning, great crowds began to arrive from the settlements and towns of Marion, Williamsburg, Darlington, Chesterfield, Marlboro, and Georgetown. These people, Confederate States citizens all, were coming to a public celebration and to watch the launching of the Confederate States Navy's newest steam warship, the *CSS Peedee*.

According to an eyewitness statement, the vessel was "a spectacle of beauty all freshly painted and sparkling in the sun. At noon the deck was filled with the crew bravely looking forward to serve the beloved Confederacy." [20]

[18] Naval War Records Office, Official Records of the Union and Confederate Navies in the War of the Rebellion, United States, Series II, Vol.II, (Government Printing Office, Washington, D.C. 1894-1922) 532
[19] Ibid, Series I, Vol. 15, 732
[20] Op. cit., Townsend, 72

South Carolina Governor A.G. Magrath, several Confederate officers, and hundreds of women looked on at the noon hour as Mrs. S. F. Gibson shattered a bottle against the bow of the vessel and said,

> " I christen this vessel *'The Peedee'* and may success attend her." The vessel slid into the murky water of the Great Pee Dee River amidst cheering from the assemble crowd at dockside. This event was followed by a picnic and a dance under one of the worksheds at the Naval Yard.[21]

Typical of a Carolina morning, the sunny day was shattered by an unexpected and brief deluge of rain before the ship's launching. Mrs. Louise Harllee Pearce of Darlington, S.C., was a young girl at the time and accompanied her family to view the launching of the new vessel.

She states that their party "was my two sisters and myself, in the carriage. In a wagon were my three younger brothers, the three Whitner boys and two Howards; two of our negro men servants to take care of the little boys and to wait upon us–and a large basket of lunch. By the time we reached Mars Bluff Ferry, it was raining hard. When we older ones decided not to try to cross the river in the open flat boat, all of the eight boys set up such cries of distress that we waited.

The river was very full–'long ferry', but when the rain stopped all of us began crossing in the open flatboat when about half way across the rain began in torrents, and all were wet to the skin.

We landed on the other side, near a fisherman's log cabin. The negro servants cut fat lightwood, made a large fire where we dried the garments of the boys–but we girls could not undress there, so we kept on our wet clothing all day.[22]

---

[21] Op. cit., Townsend, 69

[22] "Confederate Ship Never Got To Sea", Victor R. Stanley, Jr., (Charleston News & Courier, July 10, 1938)

We missed the launching, but saw the boat floating on the water and the boys enjoyed the elegant lunch." [23] Mrs. Pearce also went on to mention that businessmen, plantation owners, and ladies of the region contributed labor, funds; some of which were derived from the sale of the jewelry and silver plate contributed by the ladies; and foodstuffs to begin the building of the vessel. Because of this, it was often referred to as the ladies' gunboat.

According to an entry in Lt. Edward Means's order book dated January 12, 1864, the *CSS Peedee* was commissioned on January 11, 1864. He also notes that the river was in high freshet. The mention of exceedingly high water collaborates Mrs. Pearce's statement about the river being in 'long ferry'. [24]

CSN Lt. Oscar F. Johnston, a Virginian and formerly an officer in the United States Navy, renounced his U.S. commission and joined the Provisional Confederate States Navy at the onset of the War of Southern Independence. Prior duty assignments were to the *CSS Virginia* after the sea battle at Hampton Roads with the *USS Monitor,* command of a naval gun and crew at Drurys Bluff, service with the Submarine Defenses (mines and underwater torpedoes) under Lt. J. Pembroke Jones at Chaffins Bluff, 1st Lt. aboard the *CSS Savannah,* and commander of the blockade runner *CSS Oconee* that was lost at sea. Later promoted to 1st Lieutenant, Johnston left a teaching position as a mathematics instructor at the Confederate States school ship *CSS Patrick Henry* and accepted command of the soon to be commissioned *CSS Peedee* nearing completion at the Mars Bluff Naval Yard in early 1864. He and a complement of 90 officers and seamen assembled at the naval yard and manned the new vessel. Some of the officers assigned to Lt. Johnston's command were 2nd Lt. David Alex Telfair, CSN., a North Carolinian, 1st Lt. Charles H. Hasker, an Englishman by birth, Assistant Surgeon John H. Tucker, 2nd

[23] Op. cit., Townsend, 70
[24] Op. cit., Means, 65

Assistant Engineer R. B. Drury, 3rd Assistant Engineer W. R. Drury, 2nd Lt. John R. Price, Acting Masters Mate Charles N. Golden, and Passed Midshipman William F. Clayton, CSN.

Newly promoted 1st Lt. Charles Hazelwood Hasker had an interesting past. Born in 1831 in London, England, he was orphaned at the age of 13. As a means of supporting himself, he enlisted in the British Navy. After completing his apprenticeship, he decided to come to America. He deserted the British Navy and worked his way aboard an American ship. Upon entering the U.S., he enlisted in the U.S. Navy obtaining the rank of Boatswain and attained the rank of Lieutenant. He then was assigned aboard the *USS Susquehanna*, fell in love with a young lady from Virginia, and married. When Virginia seceded, Hasker resigned his commission in the United States Navy and offered his services to the newly formed southern nation.

He received a naval appointment as Boatswain in the Confederate States Navy. He was assigned to the newly built ironclad, the *CSS Virginia* and remained with that ship throughout the two days battle at Hampton Roads that resulted in the defeats of the Union vessels *USS Cumberland*, *USS Congress*, and *USS Monitor*. Boatswain Hasker was placed in charge of one of the forward guns aboard the Virginia. After the actions he was mentioned in dispatches from the *CSS Virginia*'s Captain Franklin Buchanan as having fought his gun well and saved the vessel from sinking by plugging a hole in the Virginia's side with oakum. Months later when the Confederate forces found it necessary to abandon the Norfolk Naval Yard and scuttle the Virginia, Boatswain Hasker was the last of the crew to leave the ship after applying the torch to the charges that destroyed the vessel.

In April of 1863, Charles Hasker was transferred to Charleston, South Carolina and assigned to the *CSS Chicora*. Promoted to Lieutenant in May of 1863, he had occasion to experience the new science of the submarine first hand.

The first successful submarine, the *CSS Hunley* was undergoing trials in Charleston Harbor. Another Lieutenant from the *CSS Chicora* had been assigned to assist aboard the new vessel in one of her practice dives. This officer became ill and being unable to go along, a volunteer was requested. Lt. Hasker tells us of this in his own words...

"I was anxious to see how the boat worked and volunteered as one of the crew to take a dive in her. We were lying astern of the steamer Etawan near Fort Johnson in Charleston Harbor. Lieutenant Payne, who had charge, got fouled in the manhole by the hawser and in trying to clear himself got his foot on the lever which controlled the fins. He had previous to this given the order to go ahead. The boat made a dive while the manholes were open and she began to fill. Payne got out of the forward hole and two others out of the after hole. Six of us went down with her. I had to get over the bar that connected the fin and through the manhole, which I did by forcing myself through the column of water that was filling the boat. The manhole plate came down on my back, but I worked my way out until my left leg was caught by the plate, pressing the calf of my leg in two and taking the skin off the shin. In this position I was carried to the bottom in forty-two feet of water. When the boat touched bottom I felt the pressure relax, and stooped down, took hold of the manhold plate, drew out my wounded limb and swam to the surface. Five men were drowned at this time. She drowned about thirty-five men in all, I being the only man saved who went to the bottom." [25]

After a stint of recovery in the hospital, Hasker returned to duty aboard the *CSS Chicora*. He assisted in the evacuation of

[25] Lt. Charles H. Hasker, His Autobiographical Note and Lecture Series. (Hasker Family Collection, South Carolina Civil War Museum, Myrtle Beach, SC)

Morris Island and in so doing, was captured by the Federal navy and sent to confinement in the Fort Warren Prison in Boston Harbor, Massachusetts. After months of confinement, he was included in an officer exchange and returned to active service. His next assignment was to the newly built *CSS Peedee*.[26]

Meanwhile, 1st Lt. Edward J. Means, CSN, a South Carolinian serving with the James River Squadron in Virginia was assigned to command the Confederate Naval Yard at Mars Bluff in late 1863. The former commander, 1st Lt. William G. Dozier, a South Carolinian, was reassigned to the James River Squadron, being relieved by Lt. Means, who took up quarters near the township of Marion Courthouse and established the headquarters for the Mars Bluff Naval Yard at Marion Courthouse. The naval records are somewhat confusing here in that there is correspondence from Lt. Van R. Morgan that indicates that he was still commanding at the Marion Courthouse Station through July of 1864. There is the possibility that both he and Lt. Means were operating a shared command as the copies of issued letters and orders that we (The CSS Pee Dee Research and Recovery Team) have found share common dates. Nevertheless, Lt. Means appears to be assuming command during this period.

There is a reference to him and his bride of four years purchasing cups and saucers at a cost of $25.00 each in Confederate currency for their new residence at the Naval Yard on the Great Pee Dee River. [27]

Lt. Means had married his third cousin and childhood sweetheart on April 18, 1860, one year and a week prior to South Carolina's firing on Fort Sumter and fifteen days after the Pony Express began its service at St. Joseph, Missouri. Means was an interesting man. Born in Fairfield, South Carolina, he attended

[26] Op. cit., Hasker.
[27] Frances Agusta Means, *The Sketch of Edward Means* (Means letters, University of SC Library, Columbia, SC) 1

the Citadel, then Annapolis, the United States Naval Academy. He served aboard the *USS Yorktown* and the *USS Jamestown*, both sailing ships. He was shipwrecked off Mayo Island near the coast of Africa. After being rescued, it appears that he returned home on leave accompanied by a large monkey he had acquired on that cruise.

One account mentions that the monkey escaped from his control during the train ride home and managed to get into the baggage car where it "scampered over trunks scaring porters." Young Means recovered his monkey and continued his journey. Upon arriving home, it seems that the "Negroes (slaves) crowded around to see him and the monkey. One old man who had been born in Africa jabbered that Marse Eddie Boy had brought one of his countrymen back. The monkey had been crouching in apparent indifference but upon seeing the African, sprang into his arms and began to look at his head. Father left the monkey at home and the family told the joke on him that if any one proposed to get rid of the troublesome beast, Aunt Sarah would protest that it reminded her so of dear little Eddie."

Means' daughter makes mention that her father was a joyous man, a lover of poetry, played the flute, an elder in the family church, chivalrous, and concerned with the well-being of others. This description would agree with his supervision of the workers at the Mars Bluff Naval Yard at a later date.

At the onset of the War for Southern Independence, Edward Means left the United States Navy. At first he served in a local militia unit, The Buckhead Guards, 6th S.C. Regiment and was wounded in the shoulder at an early battle near Dranesville, Virginia, December 20, 1861. Later Means transferred to the Provisional Navy of the Confederate States of America and assumed command of the gunboat *Beaufort* on the James River.

The family sketch prepared by his daughter continues in accuracy by stating that he was transferred to the command of the navy yard on the Peedee and continued in that command until he received orders from the Confederate Navy headquarters in Charleston to destroy the ships that he was building at the naval yard and the bridge over the Great Peedee upon Yankee General Sherman's army's approach.[28]

The daughter later makes mention that as Lt. Means and his wife were preparing to leave the Naval Yard at Sherman's approach. Means mentioned to his wife that his important papers were at the family plantation in Hampton, S.C. His wife stated that so was her jewelry as well as their silver service. They decide to return to Hampton and claim their belongings, some of which had already been looted by the Yankee soldiers that had invaded South Carolina. The daughter's statement coincides with the official records that make mention of the personnel from the naval yard being dispersed to all points until they could return to their joint command in Charleston for reassignment.[29]

Lt. Means traveled daily between the Naval Yard facilities at Mars Bluff and his headquarters at Marion Courthouse Naval Station. According to the train schedule printed for the Wilmington and Manchester Railway, travel time between Marion Courthouse and Mars Bluff was fifty-four minutes.[30] Today, this is a drive along a modern highway that requires less than ten minutes under normal driving conditions. ⇘

[28] Op. cit., Means, Frances Agusta, 1
[29] Ibid,
[30] Robert C. Black III, The Railroads of the Confederacy, (University of North Carolina Press, Chapel Hill, NC.) 4, 32, 33

Chapter 7

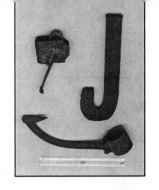

THE ACTIVITIES AT THE naval yard swelled under Lt. Means's command. Assistant Paymaster William E. Deacon, CSN., joined him at headquarters. Assistant Surgeon Hugh S. Pailey, CSN., joined the staff in late 1864. Naval Constructor E. C. Murray was assigned to the naval yard as well prior to September of 1864. By October, Thomas T. Gause's services as a machinist and engineer had been requested through the Commandant of Conscripts at Columbia, S.C. to assist in setting up several steam planing machines.

A list of some of the workmen employed at the Mars Bluff Naval Yard illustrates the wide variety of occupations utilized and their ages.

W. Hundy	38	Quarterman
W. Dickson	45	1st Rate Carpenter
Mr. Merrill	40	Blacksmith
J. C. Houston	30	2nd Rate Carpenter
J. W. Murphy	35	1st Rate Carpenter
J. S. Turner	34	1st Rate Carpenter
J. C. Pridgeon	35	1st Rate Carpenter
O. McCloud	42	2nd Rate Carpenter
J. T. Wright	25	Painter
A. Ranow	47	Fastener
W. M. Hamilton	39	2nd Rate Carpenter

J. Dorrell	46	2nd Rate Carpenter
S. M. Jenkins	46	2nd Rate Carpenter
James Castan	46	1st Rate Carpenter
W. H. Phillips	31	2nd Rate Carpenter
L. M. Sullivan	40	2nd Rate Carpenter
P. Kelley	34	1st Rate Carpenter
J. R. Jones	37	Workman
W. Davis	39	2nd Rate Carpenter
W. F. Ruby	27	1st Rate Carpenter
J. F. Finger	40	Engineer
Mr. Benson	34	2nd Rate Carpenter
S. L. Ervin	31	2nd Rate Carpenter
J. Burgess	34	1st Rate Carpenter
Thomas Paine	27	1st Rate Carpenter
O. Melton	35	2nd Rate Carpenter
C. Weatherford	40	2nd Rate Carpenter
Jo. Jones	36	Caulker
B. E. Evans	35	2nd Rate Carpenter
W. P. Collins	37	Miller
P. Morony	62	Blacksmith
B. F. Smith	36	2nd Rate Carpenter
E. C. Murray		Constructor
U. A. Morgan		Clerk
H. C. Murray		Quarterman
Calvin Dula		2nd Rate Carpenter
Wm. Sullivan		2nd Rate Carpenter
R. F. Scott		Carpenter
L. M. Twiggs		Carpenter
R. A. Booth		Carpenter
S. M. McMillan		1st Rate Carpenter
Saul Thomas		Carpenter
Charles Haselden		Pinch Operator
John Tulley		Watchman

W. L. Gregg	Watchman
D. A. Hackney	Painter
R. E. Lee	Machinist
H. G. Elliott	Carpenter
W. Johnson	Carpenter
A. H. Harrelson	Carpenter
E. G. Barnitz	Carpenter
David White	Carpenter
J. S. Thomas	Carpenter
P. Booth	Carpenter
Geo. Alexander	Laborer
Geo. Beverly	Striker
Thomas Chapman	Watchman
J. T. Gause	Machinist
Wm. Broderick	Laborer
Jo. Long	Boiler Maker
I. Beverly	Striker
Geo. Mitchell	Caulker
J. W. Carter	Carpenter[31]
Charles Haselden	Purchasing Agent
B. W. Jernigan	Shoemaker[32]

During the second year of our researching the underwater site at Mars Bluff we uncovered more broken artifacts of the Civil War period, one of them being a cobbler's broken iron shoe form. Lt. Means, concerned about the health of his laborers and their production, made every effort to see that proper rations were provided, wages were paid on time, and clothing was supplied to them.

Shortages plagued the naval yard operation. A hog cholera epidemic erupted in the Florence, Marion, and Horry district

[31] War Department Collection of Confederate Records, Section 109.12, Record Group 109, 1825-1900 (Bulk 1861-1865), Confederate Navy Department Payroll Records, Marion Courthouse Naval Station, Marion, S.C, Washington, D.C.
[32] Op. cit., Means, 21

areas and lasted for two years. This created a major shortage of meat. Lt. Means made continual requisitions for beef and pork along with flour, beans, and rice to the South Carolina Post Commissary who declined the requests stating that all of the foodstuffs in their control had been delegated to the Florence Prisoner of War Camp. Means requested subsistence from the Charleston Commissary who agreed to supply the rations. Means used the services of his purchasing agent, Charles Haselden, who had local friends and family that assisted in procuring meat for the workers at the naval yard.[33]

Cobbler's shoe form

One of the work practices at that time was for landowners and farmers to rent out their slaves as hired laborers to the various government entities. The workforce at the naval yard utilized this resource as well. The Confederate States Naval Department paid the rental fees to the slave owners and furnished rations, clothing, and living quarters for the hired workers. Lt. Means noticed that some of these men were attempting to work as loggers in the

[33] Op. cit., Means, 33

forests that surrounded the naval yard without shoes. This being an important and on-going task that furnished the pine, oak, and ash timber required by other naval facilities within the Confederate Naval Command, Means was very concerned about the safety of these workmen and of course, their production ability. The lack of shoes tended to slow production and exposed the men to hazards from serpents, splinters, axe cuts, and etc. He immediately requested that a cobbler, Mr. B. W. Jernigan, be assigned to the Mars Bluff Naval Yard. Means advised the Naval Department that he needed this man's services constantly as there was no other means of obtaining shoes for vast distances and that over eighty assorted white and black workmen depended on the services of a single shoemaker.[34]

The man was detailed to the yard as indicated by the shoe form that we discovered. Almost nineteen years later Bob Butler, Chris Amer, and I were giving a lecture to a Sons of Confederate Veterans Camp in Florence. Immediately upon finishing, a local gentleman, Mr. Randy McAllister, came over to us and introduced himself and stated that he was the great, great grandson of a Mr. Virgil Franks, an African American craftsman that worked as a cobbler at the naval yard. There is a reference to a workman named Franks in a letter from Lt. Van R. Morgan to Mr. W. A. Cummings at the Pee Dee Navy Yard wherein he is requesting payments be made to a list of workmen. His letter states that the workmen performed extra work and mentions that Franks worked Sundays through August 1, 1864. The question that surfaces is: Did both of these cobblers work together to provide footwear for the naval yard personel?

This was not the first personal touch that we encountered in our research and excavation. Midshipman Clayton's descendants live in the Florence area, one of the yard carpenters, Mr. S. M.

[34] Op. cit., Means, 26

McMillan, has family residing in Conway, S.C; and seaman Peter Vaught, Jr., a conscript from Horry District for the crew of the *CSS Peedee* also has modern day relatives in Horry County.

Throughout the twenty years of research, speaking engagements, and site exploration of the CSS Peedee Research and Recovery Team, we have found ourselves continually confronted with living associations with the artifacts that we have recovered and researched as well as the existing written records located and reviewed. It often seems that each day's work opens another window that leads into a spidery maze. The excitement of discovery never diminishes. ৯

Chapter 8

OUR UNDERWATER TEAM LED by Bob Butler by 1995 consisted of Perry Doan, James "Crunch" Wasson, Bob, Ronnie Sommersett, Debbie Butler, Chad Butler and David Bolton. Perry Doan later left us due to a heart condition and James Wasson became involved in another project. Our work continued on the site with the remaining divers. The workload had intensified as the underwater area that we were exploring was roughly a mile in length and four hundred feet wide.

Our land team of archaeologists consisted of myself, Bill Keeling, Holly Gragg-Sasser, Connie Gragg, Wiles Clemmons, and later, Stuart Pabst. There were times that interested non-team members volunteered their labor and Civil War expertise. Rod Gragg, David Jones, and John Belcner along with others aided the team. Our area of operations stretched from the railroad bridge upstream for one mile to the power line crossings on the high bluffs above the river and as far east as the eastern border of the gas pipeline right-of-way across the Great Pee Dee River. Needless to say, that is a lot of terrain. There was much work to be done. We used Fisher Research Lab's and White's Electronics metal detectors throughout the project and I have to admit that no matter how rough the environment, they never let us down.

The dive team was working in depths that varied from a few feet to as much as twenty-four feet with less than six inches of visibility. The river bottom was then and is now a maze of tangled debris, sawn logs, and ever shifting sand. The members of the dive team worked well together. Under Butler's directions they pre-planned every dive and laid a good baseline that was coordinated with our land points and central baseline. Everything was advancing and each dive uncovered new artifacts that proved the existence of the yard and the vessels built there.

One of the first activities had to be the measurements of the remnants of the shipyard's pier. This began in the summer of 1994 as we first began our artifact search at the new site. Each visit to the site of the Naval Yard and each dive yielded more information. Soon we had managed to determine the approximate size of the old pier.

Our search began to expand. The Hobby Diver Reports that were tendered to SCIAA each quarter listed the identified artifacts that were recovered from the water. Land artifacts were mapped and tagged as well and scheduled for conservation. All progressed normally and in an orderly fashion, lots of work, some excitement, and the summer wore on.

Early afternoon on August 20, 1995, I watched as the surface of the river exploded into a sudden burst of bubbles above one of the divers hidden by the muddy water. I knew then that something of importance had been discovered as the excitement below had probably resulted in a huge expulsion of oxygen from a diver. Sure enough, in a matter of moments, Bob and Ronnie surfaced. Bob removed his facemask and grinning broadly, gesticulated that there was something of importance. He and Ronnie conversed for a minute or two, then donned their masks again, and sank beneath the surface. An anxious seven or eight minutes passed before they appeared again, this time closer to the river's bank where the shallows began.

They struggled to gain a foothold and to stand under the weight of their air tanks along with whatever they were dragging in their collection basket. As they struggled up the bank those of us onshore waited with bated breath. The dive crate that they were dragging ashore broke the surface and Bob called for help. Those of us on shore waded out into the mud and assisted the divers in dragging the plastic box ashore and removing their gear. We carried the box up the hill's steep incline that bordered the site and over to Wiles Clemmons's fish cleaning shed. We had sat up a washing and identification table underneath his shed months before where we rough cleaned artifacts so that they could be tagged and recorded as to the area located and date extracted.

Whatever the object was that lay in an old blue bottled drink delivery box that Bob was using as a collection basket was squat, long, ugly, and covered with mud...besides being very heavy. I washed the mud off with the water hose and gasped. "You've done it. It's a shell from a huge artillery piece!"

Bob just grinned. "There is another one that we just placed in the shallows. Unload this and we'll bring out that one too."

While they returned for the second shell, I began to rough clean the first one. It was covered with a thick protective covering of blue clay and sand. I used a blunt scraper and a soft wire brush to remove the covering and held my breath when the first bourrelet of the artillery shell was exposed. I scrubbed more vigorously. I worked on down the shell and got to the base, discovering that the base was formed of red brass. I washed the mud from the bottom of the shell and exposed the large square nut that held the copper sabot onto the shell. This shell when identified proved beyond a doubt that there were Brooke guns at the naval yard and aboard the warship *CSS Peedee*.

Just as the team members were dragging the second shell up the steep incline, I stood the shell that I was cleaning on its end to scrub the nose and suddenly sucked in my breath. At the tip of the nose was an opening that appeared to be filled with a hard substance. Was it a fuse? I stopped cleaning so vigorously. By that time the team had reached the shed and surrounded the table, looking at and inspecting the shell that I had just cleaned.

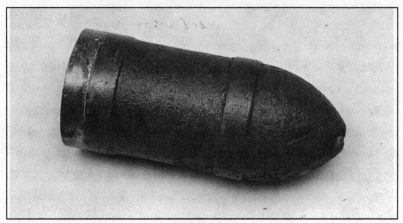

7" Brooke Shell

Several of us, including Bob, Ronnie, and myself had spent time in the military and had some familiarity with ordnance. I cautioned that the stoppage in the nose could be a fuse device or a plug. Bob agreed as well as Ronnie and I. With the team gathered around, Bob and I carefully removed the mud and impacted clay and sand from the second shell. Everything looked as the first except that this one had suffered a bit more exposure to open water and showed more distress of the iron casing. Both shells had nose openings 1½" wide that appeared to contain a hardened substance. Each shell measured 7" in diameter, 17" in height, maintained a base, a lower and an upper body bourrelet, and rested on a red brass sabot attached with a square bolt to a threaded rod that exited the base of the shell.

I selected a wooden ⅜" dowel stick, sharpened the end of it, and began to press firmly against the opening. I knew that there was a possibility that the shell was of the exploding type as it had an opening that would accommodate a fuse. What I didn't know was if the opening was blocked by some type of Borman fuse, notorious for its instability and volatility to air and probing, or if there was an earlier type of paper fuse that had decomposed. Both could be dangerous if the ignition trail was intact and there was a bursting charge within the shell's body. Black powder, the favored explosive of the Civil War period, was very volatile. A stray spark from a metallic cleaning tool or probe could initiate an explosion that could injure or kill all of us gathered around the cleaning table. I thought back to some research I'd done previously on the Brooke cannon and the published results from the Confederate Naval Ordnance works. They had stated that the Brooke shells, when fired at a range of two hundred and sixty yards from a triple banded Brooke naval rifled gun loaded with sixteen pounds of acorn black powder, would penetrate eight inches of iron plate backed with sixteen inches of white oak and then explode.[35] Interesting!

Probing the opening with a wooden dowel made good sense. As a further precaution, I asked Bob to take the water hose and keep a trickle of water running over the top of the shell just to be on the safe side in case of a stray spark. Cautiously, I pressed the dowel against the blockage and it gave way just a bit. I pressed a bit more and felt the dowel advance slightly into the aperture. Next I used a hammer and with light taps forced the dowel into the aperture. After the initial exposure it entered quite easily and a black syrupy mixture began to emerge from the top of the shell as the water seeped into the opening where the dowel had been moments before.

Bob grabbed a pan and together we tilted the shell so that the watery mixture ran out and was caught by the pan. It took about ten minutes to wash all of the black powder from the bursting cavity of the shell. We planned to save it, let the water evaporate, and see if

[35] Op. cit., Civil War Naval Chronology, 69

we could determine the chemical composition of the explosive charge. Now the two shells were safe to transport, handle, and move about. The blockage had been nothing more than the cotton tow used in the normal shipboard procedures in the mid-eighteen hundreds to prevent moisture from weeping into the explosive ordnance and fouling the shells. It had worked well....for one hundred and thirty years while the shells lay undisturbed on the river bottom after being thrown from the *CSS Peedee* before her destruction by her builders. But the ship's destruction is a later part of this story.

Several days afterward, we asked a local electronics and capacitor manufacturer, AVX inc., of Myrtle Beach to assist us by analyzing the gunpowder residue in their state of the art laboratory. They agreed to assist our team and submitted the following report:

> *"It was requested of me to confirm the composition of two samples of Confederate gunpowder. We utilized LECO (CS-444 and HF 400 carbon/sulfur and (TC-438 and EF-400) nitrogen/oxygen analyzers to determine the compositions quantitatively of the gun powder samples. We found the following results.*
>
> ***Visual inspection:*** *Rather than the typical black color associated with gunpowder, the samples had mottled brown and black coloring. Also noted was the presence of organic matter, seeds and twigs, etc.*
>
> ***Chemical anyslysis:*** *The suggested gunpowder composition was 15wt% carbon, 10wt% sulfur, and 75wt% potassium nitrate. From our elemental anyslysis we found Carbon: 55wt%, Sulfur: 5wt%, and Nitrogen/Oxygen (NO3): 40wt% but in a 1:5 ratio of nitrogen to oxygen.*

Comments: Even though the actual percentages of sulfur and nitrogen/oxygen are lower than expected, the ratio of the two are similar to the expected composition suggesting that the samples contain the gunpowder composition.

Notes: Both the potassium and nitrate have excellent solubility in water and could be readily leached by contact with water(flushing). The high carbon and oxygen levels could indicate exposure to organic compounds that would be readily available in the Pee Dee River."

On August 24 we returned to the shipyard site and diving began again. This time three shells were recovered.

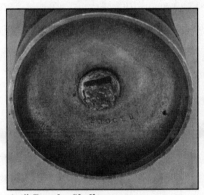

6.4" Brooke Shell   *6.4" Brooke Shell*

One was a 6.4" Brooke rifle shell, single bourrelet with a red brass sabot attached in the same way as the 7" shells. However this shell measured 6.4" in diameter, 11½" in height, and was stamped on the upper bourrelet with the initials Lt. R.D.M and RNOW. These are recognized as standing for Lieutenant Robert D. Minor who commanded the Richmond Naval Ordnance Works. This 6.4 inch specimen was also packed with cotton tow and filled with blackpowder. When I washed the mud from the bottom of this shell the running water exposed the word 'Brooke' stamped into the brass just above the large square nut that held the copper sabot onto the shell. Now there was no doubt about the type or manufacture of the ordnance aboard the Confederate vessel.

The first of the two newly recovered 7 inch shells was found to be the same as those located four days prior and was treated in the same manner for conservation preparation. However, the third one was a wee bit different in that as it lay on the ground and water was sprayed over it to wash away the fresh covering of river mud, the stream of water played upon the nose of the shell and suddenly the bright sunlight glinted evilly from the wicked looking yellow brass fuse that jutted forth from the shell.

"Bob, we've got a hot one!" I yelled. He and Ronnie rushed to my side and together, we studied the shell that literally awaited an impact to explode. This thing was somewhat safe deep in the river, but here on the bank with its fuse exposed made one aware of the danger involved in dealing with live ordnance regardless of the age of the projectile.

Bob had been a Combat Engineer and a Demolitions Expert in the Army and Ronnie a Marine. We all knelt around the shell and studied it. We decided to move the projectile cautiously to the clean up shed and inspect it from all angles. We did and once there we began cautiously to remove the encrustations from the shell. Using an old toothbrush and a rag, we worked slowly and easily on the surface of the fuse, searching for a way to disarm this thing without endangering any of our fellow workers or us.

Ronnie stopped his brushing and pointed toward the base of the fuse. "Bob, look there. Is that a safety wire protruding from the fuse base?"

Bob and I both looked close and sure as shooting, there was an intact brass wire shaped like an elongated carter pin that passed through the base of the fuse.

Bob spoke first. "I'll bet that passes beneath the striker and serves as a stop between the striker and an igniter."

He knew more about this than I did but I nodded sagely anyway. "I can remove that fuse!" He said.

Ronnie and I drew in deep breaths.

"You serious?" I looked at him incredulously.

"I'll help!" Ronnie said.

"Y'all worry me!" Was my comment; and with that I took the other three team members present and sought cover behind a nearby brick wall like it would really protect us from an explosion.

Bob proceeded in his operation. He picked up a rag and an adjustable wrench from a nearby table and placed the rag around the fuse to protect it; checked again to make sure that the safety wire was intact, motioned for Ronnie to hold the shell steady, placed the adjustable wrench on the rag over the widest part of the fuse's body and gave a mighty jerk on the wrench.

My heart stopped. No explosion. "It turned." Bob simply said.

I left the brick wall and came closer to watch, curiosity taking over. Bob applied less pressure this time. We could all see the fuse rotate.

One turn, a turn and a half, two turns, then three…and a shrieking piercing whistle sounded from the shell like all the demons from Hell had been loosed at once. All that I could think of was the word "Incoming!" I turned and made a beeline back for the brick wall. I looked over my shoulder just as I left the ground in my dive for cover and saw Ronnie and Bob still perched around that projectile looking as calm as ever.

Seconds passed. The whistling abated. There was no explosion. Sheepishly, the three of us came from behind the brick wall to stare in amazement at our two intrepid companions. Their response was simply to say "Y'all scared or something?"

7" Brooke shell with the live fuse

Now that time has passed we all know that the gaseous buildup of the decaying powder over time created a vast amount of pressure that had been contained within the shell by the fuse. Once the fuse had been backed away from the shell by turning just a few of the large pipe threads in the fuse holder, that built up gas had begun to leak out under pressure, creating the disturbing sound. Nevertheless, it just goes to show that an Army engineer and a Marine are immune to loud and disturbing noises.

Other dive reports from this period reflect various items recovered for research…a 19th century mustard bottle, a harmonica, coal, crockery shards, machine parts and a drive wheel, logging cleats, lead slag, peach seeds, nails, screws, canister shot, a logging pike, metal inspectors stamp with the raised letter 'V', files small and large, grape shot, countersink bits, 19th century lead pencil, sword scabbard drag, anchor chain, hooks, broken parts of the cook stove from the ship's galley, sail grommets, files, a caulkers mallet, ship's windlass, brass bearing sleeves, a broken pocket knife, and a 19th century shoe.

These same dive reports reflect the instruments used in the dives. Common items mentioned are metal detectors, compasses, transits, draftsman's tools, assorted scuba gear like air tanks, masks, a water dredge, dry suits, wet suits, and communication sets.

Each day's objective was reported as well. This might be as simple as selecting a particular section of grid and running metal detectors over that portion of the sub-surface or mapping out a specific grid site to link up with the base line and prior mapping projects, or locating a suspected and important feature like the pillars and pilings of the yard's dock or inspecting the underwater foundation structure of the suspected power wheel station. All of these tasks and more had to be accomplished...Where did the ferry slip begin and end, was there a sluice gate to a wet area in the lower naval yard section? How far did the dock extend into mid-stream and how long was it? Are there other magnetic anomalies? Many days were spent in triangulation of known artifacts within the gridded areas along with the tagging of the recovered sampled artifacts.

Overlying items were also noted, collected, and recorded. Some of the modern objects accumulated were a .30 caliber bullet, a .45 acp bullet weighing 230 grains, 14 beer tabs (same spot, same day), two lead sinkers (one salt water and one fresh water), a commode, a Pepsi bottle, a doorknob, and a broken fishing rod. Each day's work required identification and removal of modern items. These things indicated the amount of modern habitation and usage of the river.

The water conditions were noted as well and very often under additional comments one will find phrases reading "snakes out today...many snakes encountered underwater, unexpected flotsam, extremely hot, little or no air movement over the channel, etc." One interesting comment made on the July 14, 1996 report mentions that a boat structure seems to be uncovered. After reviews of this particular area, most of the team was convinced that the remains of one of the frames of a torpedo boat being built at the yard might still be in existence. There were two torpedo boats constructed at the Mars Bluff Naval Yard. One was completed and launched with an engine being installed on her that had been sent from the cargo imported by the blockade runner *South*

Carolina. This is referenced in Lt. Means's order book several times. [36, 37]

Confederate General P. G. T. Beauregard was the commander of the Department of South Carolina and Georgia during the 1862-1864 period. He approved and encouraged on-going construction of warships from his headquarters in Charleston, S.C., favored development of new submersible types of vessels, and believed in a unified command between the army and naval forces in his district. He encouraged new ideas and scientific advances in naval vessels and operations.

One of his junior officers was Captain Francis D. Lee, an ingenious young engineer who developed a torpedo that when attached to a long spar or pole would explode when rammed into the hull of an enemy ship. In order to carry this weapon to the enemy, he designed a steam powered semi-submergible vessel that lay low in the water, with only its smokestack, the pilots' cockpit, and the rounded top of its armored deck breaking the water line. These vessels were relatively easy to build, low in expense, and promised great devastation against the blockaders that surrounded the Southern coasts. [38]

Lt. Means tells of two, possibly three, of these vessels being built at the Mars Bluff Naval Yard. After the war, Union Ensign Sturgis Center also makes mention of steam engines for these vessels being on shore at the Naval Yard. [39]

This wreck has not been verified at this time and require further inspections and investigations to confirm that it is one of the torpedo boats being constructed at the Mars Bluff Naval Yard. ⟋

[36] Op. cit., *Means*, 60
[37] Ibid, 75
[38] Op. cit., Still, Jr. , 13, 17
[39] Op. cit., Center

Debbie Butler on sorting dock

Holly Gragg Sasser snake watching

L-R: Chris Amer SCIAA;
Lynn Harris, SCIAA

L-R: Chris Amer SCIAA;
Ronnie Summersett- PDTeam
James "Crunch" Wasson - PD Team
Joe Beatty, SCIAA

Ted Gragg and maps

L-R: Connie and Ted Gragg on rope

Connie Gragg: Listing divers recovered artifacts

L-R: Ted Gragg; Bob Butler

Chad Butler with sifting scoop and artifact pail at naval yard

L-R: Bob Butler in dive gear assisted by David Bolton aboard dive boat

Ted and Connie Gragg at mapping table

Ted Gragg on dive boat

Bob Butler inspecting artifacts at PeeDee wreck site

L-R: Bob Butler, Ted Gragg and Ronnie Sommersett

Chapter 9

BUT WHAT OF THE ship *CSS Peedee*? Her mission was simple; interdict the United States warships off the coast of South Carolina, pierce their blockade, and then what? Escape to sea to become a commerce raider like the *CSS Alabama*? Maybe. There are some interesting comments in Lt. Edward Mean's order book. One is an early copy of correspondence written on September 17, 1864. In this letter, Lt. Means reports that the two rifled guns (Brooke cannon) had been shipped from Augusta, Georgia, on the 8th of September, the carriages for those rifled guns were due at the Mars Bluff Naval Yard not later than the 18th of September, and that the ordnance stores for those guns were at Kingsville and due in on the next train to arrive at the Peedee Community railroad depot. Means goes on to say that "the mast is up and rigged." [40] Thus begins the first of many historical arguments concerning the number of masts on the gunboat. The vessel was depicted on the monument stone at the Florence Library as having three masts when the propellers were placed on exhibit in the 1920s.

Former Passed Midshipman W. F. Clayton, formerly of the *CSS Peedee* states that the vessel was schooner rigged. Schooner rigging is a term for a sailing ship that usually mounts two masts with the forward mast either being shorter or the same height as the aft or rear mast. The rigging usually extends from the bowsprit

[40] Op. cit., Means, 24

with a martingale to the stem, a foremast stay, a jib and stay foresail, a fore-gaft topsail, a foresail and mainstays, a main-gaff topsail, a main sail, and a boom end.

This just adds to the confusion as the term 'schooner rigged' can apply to any vessel carrying two to six masts. Everything seems to center around the presence of a mainsail mast; our supposition is that the vessel had two masts, with the aft or main mast being taller and the one that Lt. Means refers to when he mentions that the mast is in place. The boiler's funnel would have been somewhere between the fore and aft mast.

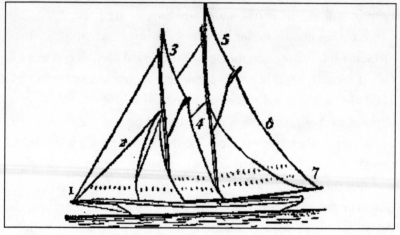

Schooner Rigging

1: bowsprit, with martingale to the stem; 2: fore-topmast-stay, jib and stay-foresail; 3, fore-gaff-topsail; 4: foresail and mainstays; 5: main-gaff-topsail; 6: mainsail; 7: end of boom.

Interestingly, the design of the *CSS Chattahoochee*, a sister ship designed by Constructor John L. Porter, partially raised and on exhibition at the Port Columbus Civil War Naval Museum in Columbus, Georgia, illustrates a similarly built wooden warship sporting three masts, schooner rigged. In comparison, besides the questions concerning the masts aboard the vessel, the question also arises about the overall mission and design of the *CSS*

Peedee. Was she to be used to protect the inland and coastal waters of South Carolina or was she to join the ranks of the exalted, the Confederate Cruisers of the *Alabama* class?

Secretary of the Navy in mid-1863 directed that the steamer *Peedee* be fitted with large freshwater tanks. And later the Confederate States Navy Secretary Mallory stated in a report dated November 30, 1863, "that one seagoing steam gunboat of five guns is advancing to completion on the Pee Dee River in South Carolina". The key words in this statement are 'seagoing steam gunboat'.[41] Lt. Means makes mention of this in a letter dated October 25, 1864 to Chief Naval Constructor Porter who at that time was in Wilmington, N.C. Means asks if Porter will come up to the Mars Bluff Naval Yard to 'suggest the necessary alterations' as the builders are going to have to cut up the berth deck of the *Peedee* to install the requested water tanks.[42]

One can only surmise at the reasoning behind this request for additional freshwater tanks; that being the vessel was to go to sea. When the ship was on inland fresh waters, the boilers could utilize the water resource that floated the vessel. However, going to sea or being in brackish water created a mass of problems; the first of which was the corruption of the boiler tubes when using sea water, called burn out, by the salt left after the evaporation of the sea water. Salt water also produced less energy resulting in a slower speed for the vessel. Converting sea water to fresh water was possible through several known methods of distillation of the sea water into fresh water; however, these methods all required heat which when created required the expenditure of fuel, thus creating a need to carry more coal, and therefore increasing the need for additional storage space and creating more weight that in turn required more energy to move the vessel.

---

[41] Op. cit., Official Records of the Union and the Confederate Navies, Series I, Vol. 13, 692
[42] Op. cit., Means, 24

The continued use of sea water for the boilers of an early 1860s warship was a Catch-22 situation. Extended sea cruises demand better and longer performance of engines and boilers without shore based maintenance. In the early 1860s, the triple expansion steam engine had not been developed. The triple expansion method allows the same steam to be utilized several times and then condensed to restore fresh water. But at the time of the Civil War, this technology wasn't available. The engines of that time utilized the steam as an immediate resource without replenishment so there was a demand for a larger reserve of fresh water. Thus the need for additional fresh water...and we suppose that the extra tanks were added to solve this dilemma. Further, when adding the extra tanks, it became necessary to remove one of the three masts. This was done, the tanks added, and the ship was commissioned, our team thinks, with two masts only, not three, just the two.

And to go further in thought, we suspect that the aft mast was the taller of the two and this is the mast that Lt. Means mentions. The supposition of the need for the fresh water tanks also lends credence to the Confederate States Navy Secretary's comments that the *Peedee* was to be an ocean raider and also lends support to Union Admiral Dahlgren's preparations for her interception to prevent her from escaping to sea.

On October 27 Lt. Means wrote Secretary of the Navy Mallory and stated that Constructor Porter declined coming to the Mars Bluff Naval Yard for the proposed meeting. Means went on to state that he intends to direct the yard's naval constructor E. C. Murray to make the best arrangements for it (the freshwater tank) under the circumstances.[43]

Next comes the question of the spelling of the name of the vessel. Period accounts and correspondence between the officers assigned to the Mars Bluff Naval Yard, the *CSS Peedee*, and the

[43] Op. cit., Means, 27

Marion Courthouse Naval Station as well as interested citizens illustrate the usage of both spellings of the name *Pee Dee*. Some refer to the ship as the *Pee Dee* while others use the spelling *Pedee*, and still others use *Peedee*. Then there is the question of the *Peedee's* dimensions. John L. Porter's original plans called for this class of gunboats, the Macon Class, to be 150 feet in length, twin screw driven. Another reference, the Civil War Naval Chronology, states that the *Peedee* was to be 170' in length, with a beam of 26', and draw 10 feet of water.[44] Still another source suggests 130' in length, 30' beam, and 10' of draw, or maybe 150' in length with a beam of 25' and a draw of 8'.[45]

Confederate Navy Lt. Van R. Morgan stated in his letter of May 1863 from the Marion Courthouse Naval Station that the gunboat being constructed under his supervision is 150' in length, with a beam of 25', and drawing 7½' on the high sea.[46] This is interesting in that he gives the basic measurements of the Macon Class vessels designed by Constructor Porter and in the same sentence uses the phrase 'on the high sea'. It would seem that this information from the assigned commandant of the Naval Yard where the vessel was being built would be the best estimate for the ship's measurement and her intended mission.

And, if those controversies are not enough, then there are the arguments about the warship's armament. One reference, The Civil War Navy Chronology, details that the *Peedee* was to mount a battery of four 32 pounders in broadside and two 9" pivot guns.[47] Another reference suggests four 32 pounders broadside, one 32 pounder rear, and one 9" pivot.[48] Secretary of the Navy Mallory stated that in April 1864, the steam sloop *Peedee* was

---

[44] Op. cit., *Civil War Naval Chronology*, Vol. 6, 281
[45] Op. cit., Clayon, 218
[46] Op. cit., Morgan
[47] Op. cit., *Civil War Naval Chronology*, Vol. 6, 281
[48] Op. cit., Clayon, 218

completed with four heavy guns.[49] Then, to further confound the issue, Union Rear-Admiral Dahlgren, U.S. Navy, reports in a dispatch dated October 29, 1864, that the "*Pedee* should be down (to Winyah Bay) soon and her battery is composed of eight guns, two of which are 10" cannon." Just a few months later on February 6, 1865, that the ship *Pedee* (notice the name spelling) was coming down the river bearing a battery of two rifled 32 pounders and a Whitworth gun.[50] Finally, going back in time a year or so, the Confederate commander of the Mars Bluff Naval Yard, Lt. Morgan, in a letter dated May 1863, states that the intended armament of the ship under construction at the naval yard is a battery of four guns, 32 and 42 pounders.[51]

Fortunately, we had a few better clues as to the armament of the *CSS Peedee*. These correct tidbits came from the naval yard commander's order book, from the records of the Confederate Naval Foundry at Selma, Alabama, as well as information on the gun carriages from the Charlotte, N.C. Confederate naval manufacturing facility, and from information gained concerning the Confederate Ordnance Works in Richmond, Va.

The Selma Foundry shipped two Brooke rifled guns, serial numbers S46 and S53 to the Mars Bluff Naval Yard. Gun number S46, a 7" bore Brooke rifle, shipped to Peedee, S.C. on July 3, 1864. This gun had been cast and completed on April 12, 1864.

Manufacturing and completing a 7" double-banded Brooke rifle was an arduous task. This type of naval gun weighed 14,000 pounds. Number 1 or Number 2 cold blast pig iron was tapped from reverberating furnaces. After the metal was fused, the molten iron was poured into a gun mold. The filled mold was then placed into a pit to cool for eight to ten days. Afterward, the cast-

---

[49] Op. cit., *Official Records of the Union and Confederate Navies*, Series I, Vol.15, 732
[50] Ibid, Series 1, Vol. 16, 219
[51] Op. cit., Morgan

ing was removed from the mold and sent to a boring mill. The boring of the barrel of the gun could take up to 900 hours of intensive labor. After the boring was completed the gun tube was rifled. This took another 13 hours  or so, turned in a lathe for 31 more hours. Then the protruding trunnions were finished. This was accomplished in 20 hours or so. The next operation was the attaching of the inner and outer Brooke bands. This phase required 52 hours. The bands were expanded by heating and then slipped into place on the cold barrel to harden and shrink into place. After this, the gun was sighted, the cascabel attached, and the barrel vented for the ignition primers. On the average, one Selma Brooke 7" gun took 3 months to complete with laborers working around the clock to finish the task.[52]

Ten days later, gun number S53, another Brooke rifle bored in 6.4" shipped to Peedee, S.C. This gun was new also and had been poured on April 29, 1864.

The records from the Selma Naval Foundry indicate that George Veitch and his assistants moulded Gun number S53 in seven sections of flasks. The mold was heated in the oven for 48 hours. 15,000 pounds of Bibb cold blast pig iron number 1 and number 1 low order was used; in fact it was melted nine times in the number 3 furnace at Selma and poured into the mold on the 29th of April, 1864. The gun tube blank was hoisted out of the mold on May 5 after cooling for six days and sent to the boring mill on May 7. The gun head was removed as well that day, and after four boring stages, the metal was examined for crystallization and color. The muzzle was faced on May 9. The measurement of the bore was 118. 5 inches, including the 7" diameter breech

[52] Op. cit., Daniel, Riley, 75, 82, 83

chamber. The trunnions were finished on May 28, the inner bands were mounted and allowed to shrink into place on June 16, and the outer bands were installed four days later. By June 22, the turning had been finished. The sighting and elevator were installed by June 27, the barrel was fully rifled by July 2, and the cascabel block was finally attached and fitted on July 9, 1864. Three days later it was on the way to join the new pride of the Confederate States Navy, the *CSS Peedee*.[53]

Lt. Means mentions in a dispatch of September 17, 1864, that he has received communication that the two rifled guns for the *Peedee* had shipped from Augusta, Georgia, on the 8th of September and should be arriving at the Naval Yard.[54] The gun carriages had shipped from Charlotte, N.C., and should arrive at the Naval Yard on the 18th of September. A special messenger from Richmond, Virginia, had arrived that day at Marion Courthouse Naval Station and reported that the ordnance stores were at Kingsville, S.C., and should be at the Mars Bluff Yard on the next train. The two rifled guns arrived at the Naval Yard on September 24, 1864.

The final gun to arrive for use on the *CSS Peedee* was a 9" captured Dahlgren cannon. This gun was numbered on the breech FP 573 and marked on the left trunnion with the initials JMB. The initials JMB are those of John M. Berrien, the ordnance officer at the Fort Pitt Foundry 1862 through 1864. These markings indicate that the large cannon had been cast at the Fort Pitt Foundry, Pittsburg, Pennsylvania, in the United States of America, in mid 1862. Prior to the onset of the Civil War, this foundry was known as Knap, Rudd, & Company. With the advent of war, this became the Fort Pitt Foundry & Artillery Proving Grounds.

---

[53] Op. cit., Babits, Harris, Caudell, Edmonds, 79
[54] Op. cit., Means, 1

These large 9" Dahlgren smoothbore guns were used as heavy battering artillery. The gun in question had been salvaged by the Confederate Navy after sinking a Union vessel that mounted one of these large cannons. It is suspected that this gun was aboard the *USS Southfield*, a Yankee gunboat rammed and sunk by the Confederate States Ram *CSS Albemarle*. This action occurred in the Roanoke River during the battle of Plymouth, April 19, 1864. The gun was raised from the wreck, cleaned, inspected, and shipped to Mars Bluff Naval Yard where it was installed aboard the *CSS Peedee*.

Never the less, Dahlgren gun number 573, as it was cast in mid 1862, was not among the captured Union guns from the seized Federal naval facilities at Norfolk, Virginia on April 20, 1861. That being the case, it had to have been recovered from one of the United States vessels that was sunk by Confederate ships of war. The *USS Southfield*, *The USS Eastport*, and the *USS Indianola* were the three sunken warships that mounted these massive guns. As the Indianola and the Eastport wrecks lay in the western theater waters, it is more likely that the IX Dahlgren was recovered from the wreck of the *USS Southfield*.[55]

Lt. Means's order book confirms the addition of the 9" Dahlgren gun. In a letter to Secretary Mallory on October 27, 1864, Means states that he has not made the changes to the hatches and the bulwarks of the *Peedee* yet as ordered by Mallory to give free play to the 9" gun as he is still waiting the new chasse for the gun to arrive to prevent any construction mistakes.[56] Means informed Mallory again on November 11 that Chief Naval Constructor Porter recommends shifting the pivots for the 9" gun. The Charlotte Naval Yard sent instructions as well to lengthen the chasses and this

[55] Lawrence E. Babits, "Confederate Artillery Material from the PeeDee River", SC. Military Collector's and Historian's, Journal of the Company of Military Historians Vol 63, No 1
[56] Op. cit., Means, 27

would necessitate cutting the hatches. Another telegram to Secretary Mallory on the 11th of November corrected the former missive and stated that the gun carriage maker from Charlotte, N.C. had arrived with directions to increase the 9" chasse. Porter has also advised to change the shifting pivots and this will require only a small portion of the forward hatch to be cut away. [57]

Not only do these dates collaborate a suspected time line between recovery of the 9" gun from the wreck of the *USS Southfield* and its delivery to Mars Bluff; they also illustrate that the 9" amidships gun that Passed Midshipman Clayton manned was placed directly behind the forward hatch.

Interestingly, the report of the nine-inch ammunition arriving on September 26, 1864, indicates an even faster acquisition time for the 9" gun. [58]

This class of Union gun had a trunnion diameter of 7.25", 131.5 " in length, and weighed 9200 pounds. ∫

[57] Op. cit., Means, 35, 38
[58] Ibid, Means, 10

Chapter 10

IT WAS SEPTEMBER 17, 1995. I had just finished metal detecting the area at the rear of the old pier about 800 yards upstream from the railroad bridge. I was searching for slag or iron particulate that would substantiate my theory of a forge and piglets in the area. It was hot and dry. My thoughts were of a cool Coca-Cola in the cooler that rested on Wiles Clemmons' dock.

Soon afterward, having reached the dock and secured a cold soda from the cooler, I sat down on the old wooden bench at the end of the dock and leaned against the railing, savoring the refreshing coolness trickling down my throat as I gazed across the river's expanse. A sudden burst of bubbles caught my attention as Bob Butler poked his head out of the water and searched the surroundings to get his bearings. He looked at the compass on his wrist and laying on his back, shuffle paddled toward the ladder attached to the dock.

I stood up, waiting for him to grasp the base of the ladder and rest a bit before beginning the fifteen foot climb to the dock's floor. This time he didn't even shake his tanks loose. Instead here he came, up the ladder, hand over hand.

"Give me a hand up." He said as he reached the next to the last rung.

"What's up?" I grabbed his hand and pulled upward. He clambered through the rail opening and started shrugging his shoulders from the harness that supported the weight of the scuba tank. He dropped the rig to the floor of the dock and unfastened his weight belt. Straightening and stretching from the weight of the discarded gear, he removed the flippers from his feet and sat down on the bench.

"Long dive." Was all he said.

I waited. I expected more. Bob and I had been together quiet awhile now and we were used to each others' expressions and moods.

His mouth twitched ever so slightly into an almost grin. "You know where the 'Wait A Minute Log' is, right?"

I nodded. The 'Wait A Minute Log' was the Team's polite moniker for the profane name that had been given to a huge underwater monster that all the divers struck their head against if they missed the tied warning knot in the guide rope that we had labeled Highway Number 1 as a nasty reminder of the Nam.

"Well, it's right there just upstream from it, from the 'Wait a Minute Log'," Bob said, still trying to hold back a grin.

"What's right there?" I couldn't fathom what he was talking about.

"One of the cannons you keep wishing that we would find!" he said.

My mouth must have hit my shoes because he laughed. Finally, after all of these years, without a doubt, Butler had done it. They were here, those cannons. Well, at least one. It is impossible to describe our excitement. So many before us had failed to find any sign of the guns from the *CSS Peedee*. Now we had shells and a cannon. Pretty good proof. Yep, pretty good proof.

Bob went further. "I claimed it for us in case there ever is a question."

"How did you accomplish that?" I asked.

"Easy. I brushed the sand off of it enough to expose the muzzle.

I had a quarter with me in my dive bag. I recorded the date on it a while back after we found the shells just in case we found a gun. Today I placed the quarter as far as I could reach down the muzzle of that thing."

"How big is the gun?" I was still pretty excited.

"The muzzle's got to be at least eight inches in diameter," Bob said. "I couldn't touch the sand inside the tube. It was further than the length of my arm. So I placed the quarter in it and added more sand into the muzzle. I think that it is there to stay. There is a lot of the barrel exposed, but it seems to be lying on its side."

That evening we called a team meeting and planned the next week's dive. It would be necessary to chart and inspect the cannon from the muzzle to the cascabel. We didn't have any underwater photography equipment. But we had good lights, bright tape measures, and an intense attitude of "We can do it." Bob came up with the idea of using a strong oiled paper and a heavy carpenter's pencil to trace out any numbers or letters that they found on the gun. This part of the project and the continued search for the other cannon of the warship as well as continued exploration of the river's bottom and the surrounding landmass occupied much of the next twelve months. A year and one week later we undertook a new approach to the intensive survey with the permission of SCIAA.

The CSS Peedee Research and Recovery Team assembled at the river site early on the morning of July 28, 1996. The goal for the day's work was to map and record the gun tube that Bob had found and also look for any indication of the carriage. Ronnie Sommersett, Bob Butler, and David Bolton would make the descent.

Chris Amer at SCIAA had asked us to divest the gun of its sand and clay covering so that correct measurements could be made of the cannon. We ordered a gasoline pumping system from California for this purpose along with enough 4" hose to reach the bottom of the river. While we waited on the pump system to arrive, Bob and Chad built a ten foot square flotation dock that was mounted on 55 gallon barrels that served as flotation devices to support the pump equipment. We were about to use a water dredge on the site for the first time. And, to uncover and measure a cannon, that if all were as we hoped, would turn out to be one of the guns from the *CSS Peedee* and not a cannon left on the bank after the destruction of the Naval Yard.

The morning's work began in earnest. The divers entered the water and advanced up river until they had reached the marked location between baseline points F & G. They worked steadily in the dark void beneath the surface with the hose from the water dredge. Clouds of mud and sand rose rapidly through the dark water of the Great Pee Dee River. A water dredge works like a vacuum cleaner except that instead of an exchange of air, its moving force is created by compression of available water and its dispersion through a hose to the covered object. Debbie, Connie, and I watched from the dock as the fevered expulsion of bubbles breaking the river's surface illustrated the activities beneath the water.

Ted and Connie Gragg at drafting table plotting location of recovered artifacts on chart.

On the drafting table, I had drawn the first elements of the day's chart...that being the base line and coordinates along with the measurements from point to point beginning at Point A and ending at H. The protractor, ruler, and T-square lay on the table, waiting. It seemed like an eternity passed before the divers surfaced. Shortly they had joined us on the dock, shed their gear, and began making their reports as I charted them on the grid.

Their findings that day confirmed the findings made last year when SCIAA's team and ours inspected the guns; that's right, guns, again. Later we found the others, but that story comes a bit later. David had traced out the letters found on one of the 9 inch gun's trunnions...JMB...the very same letters that you can clearly see today on the film taken underwater fourteen years later, in June of 2010.

On that day, fourteen years ago, we measured the overall gun's length from cascabel to the muzzle at 147 inches, exactly 134 inches from the breech base of the gun to the muzzle, with a muzzle diameter of roughly nine inches. The trunnions measured 7.5" in diameter. The gun rested on its side at a 37 degree angle with the muzzle pointing toward Point G on the baseline. All of the divers said that the metal appeared to be in very good condition as exemplified by the tracing of the trunnion's letters; they being very clear.

Two items were found near the cascabel of the Dahlgren...a wooden wedge measuring 1.5" in width at the narrow end and 3" in width at the wide end, with a length of 7". The sides were tapered and the thickness of the wedge was ¾". A friction primer was recovered alongside the cascabel. A large lump of coal weighing twenty pounds was found near the breech of the gun. Further back toward point E one of the divers located a chisel and a ring cleat, a 6" nail, a stranded piece of wire , and a bent forged nail along with an open-sided cleat.[59]

One week and eleven years passed after the location of the 9" Dahlgren before our team found the 6.4" Brooke. Bob Butler found the Brooke 6.4 gun on September 23, 2006. It lay almost in a direct line thirty-six feet further north of the 9" gun. We had narrowed the search area by estimating the distance between the shipboard

[59] Connie B. Gragg and Ted L. Gragg, Grid map, July 7/28/1996, CSS Peedee Research and Recovery Team, SCIAA

mounting of the 6.4" Brooke rifle from the 9" amidships gun. Early after finding the 9" gun, and for years following, we analyzed data, took readings, and studied the structure of warships of the 1860 period. The team visited museums and measured existing cannons and carriages in an attempt to correctly determine the amount of space and exact placement of these large naval guns and chasses on warship decks. Our magnetic readings with the metal detectors indicated a large anomaly approximately 37 feet north of the 9" gun and in toward the eastern shore. But eleven long years would pass before we found this Brooke cannon and verified the existence of this gun by hands-on examination. The gun in question sits with the muzzle pointing upward at the surface, the tube is exposed for almost six feet, and the trunnions and bands appear to be supporting the gun in an upright position being bound by a current stacked log jam and tons of sand.

There are large chunks and blocks of steam coal present around the gun. This may suggest that the ships coaling bunkers were off loaded in this area before the 6.4" Brooke was pushed off the chasse and over the rail of the Peedee.

Many things had happened during those eleven years. William Keeling had died after a two year battle with cancer. David Bolton had moved out of the area, Ronnie and Perry had suffered heart attacks with Ronnie's first attack being on site during a dive. In addition, many grandchildren had been born, and Bob and Debbie had married.

I had the honor of performing their wedding ceremony and if you have never been a guest at a scuba wedding, you have no idea of what you are missing. Imagine, if you will, instead of uniformed officers with an arch of swords for the bride and groom to pass through, an intrepid group of divers form an arch by hoisting their swim fins overhead as the matrimonial couple pass beneath the variously colored diving fins.

The next item on the agenda as to cannon was to locate the last and third gun. Again we estimated the length of the chasse and tube of the gun and its possible placement near the bow and began an exhaustive search with the underwater metal detectors. Several large anomalies appeared in this area. After careful examination of two of the larger massed readings, we concluded that the third gun lay 139 feet above the amidships gun and was buried under at least nine feet of cut timbers and sunken logs. Exposing this gun would be a massive project. Therefore we charted the supposed position and elected to continue to exam the area of the first Intensive Survey permit.

But wait a minute. There could be more. Remember! There was a reference to two brass howitzers, each a 24 pounder, that were received at the Mars Bluff Naval Yard on December 26, 1864, from Selma, Alabama. In a letter to Commander J. M Brooke, Lt. Means states that he understood that one was to be mounted on the *Peedee* and the other used to guard the Naval Yard. He makes mention that no carriages accompanied these guns and that he needed to know where those were to have originated.[60] This reference continued to nag at us. Too many instances kept pointing to the possibility of other cannon aboard the ill-fated vessel...the earlier mentions in dispatches about 24 and 32 pounders along with the knowledge that Lt. Means confirmed their existence. Sadly, to date, we still have no knowledge of the whereabouts of these guns. They may have been shipped elsewhere in the final days of the war, taken to Cheraw, S.C., when the ordnance stores from the Mars Bluff site were evacuated, or gathered and sold for scrap during the World War I scrap drives for brass and bronze items. They may still exist today as one of the vast array of magnetic anomalies beneath the bed of the modern day Great Pee Dee River. ⟩

[60] Op. cit., Means, 61

Chapter 11

THE *CSS PEEDEE'S* PROPULSION system was primarily steam with wind or sail power as an auxiliary means that under ideal conditions would add several knots to her expected speed. Movement through the water was accomplished by the action of two massive bronze propellers of a new and radical pitch and design. These were engineered and manufactured in England and shipped across the Atlantic by one of the blockade runners. The vessel's engines again are somewhat argumentative. Some records claim that the engines came through the blockade, while others say that the ship mounted one engine built in Richmond and one that was manufactured in England. Secretary of the Confederate Navy Stephen Mallory asserted in a departmental report of November 30, 1863, that both engines mounted aboard the *CSS Peedee* were built by the Confederate Naval Iron Works at Richmond, Virginia. He went on to make mention of the fact that at their maximum settings, the boat would make about nine knots under steam as the engines were designed for a smaller boat but were used on the larger *Peedee* when circumstances prevented the smaller vessel from being completed.[61]

The ship was large, very large for the river that served as its birthplace. Regardless of the true size of the vessel, either 150 feet or 170 feet in length, and with a beam of 25 to 28 feet, she would

[61] Op. cit., *Official Records of the Union and Confederate Navies*, Series 1, Vol 13, 733.

occupy a lot of space on the winding Great Pee Dee River. In the reaches of the river above the railroad bridge, the narrow channel would make navigational turns almost impossible. The prevailing thought at the time of the War Between the States was that the Great Pee Dee River was impassable for ships travelling upstream from Winyah Bay, that is unless they mounted double engines that could be useful in steering due to the narrow and twisting turns of the river's channel. Voyages upstream also required a higher rate of speed to overcome the river's fast current as it sped toward the sea. On the other hand, a vessel with the estimated nine knot speed of the *CSS Peedee* could complete the downstream journey of a 100 miles or so in less than a day.

Early in the conflict between the two nations, the United States Navy invaded Port Royal Sound and seized Hilton Head, South Carolina. After the investment of Port Royal Sound by Federal forces, a large naval station was built at Hilton Head for the refueling, coaling, and repair of Union vessels engaged in the blockade of the Southern ports. This area also served as a transfer point for Union troops in movement to various theatres of the war and an exchange and transfer point for prisoners of war.

Rear Admiral John A. B. Dahlgren commanded the South Atlantic Blockading Squadron from July of 1863 through the end of the War Between the States. He was aware of the construction of the *CSS Peedee*, the Mars Bluff Naval Yard, and of course the railroad crossing near Florence as well as the Confederate prisoner of war stockade in Florence. The Union army possessed a huge desire to free these 10,000 or so Union prisoners interred at Florence. This desire was known to the Confederate forces as well and concerned the local military commanders greatly. Lt. Edward Means, commander of the Marion Courthouse Naval station was one of these officers concerned with the affairs emanating from the Florence stockade and the threat that was posed by its inmates.

Unknown to both Lt. Means and Rear-Admiral Dahlgren, both men were on a collision course with destiny.

In a communication dated September 17, 1864, Lt. Means "earnestly requests that the officers and crew (of the *Peedee*) be sent as soon as possible for several thousand Yankee prisoners have been sent to Florence, S.C. which is only ten miles from the Yard and as the country is entirely unprotected a raid may be made any day for their release and to destroy the Yard, Gun Boat, and Rail Road Bridge".[62]

Means also telegraphed Secretary Mallory that "six thousand Yankee prisoners are now in Florence, S.C. and I am told the number is to be increased to ten thousand. Florence is only ten miles from the Navy Yard and the prisoners being there makes it a great point of interest. There are only five companies defending the coast from Georgetown to the North Carolina line and a raiding party would be able in one night to destroy the Gun Boat, Navy Yard, and Rail Road Bridge which is not more than one hundred and fifty yards from the yard. I have the workmen drilled three times a week but as there is a good deal of sickness among them they will not muster more than thirty-five or forty at any time. I have informed General Chestnut that I will have to keep them at the Yard for the protection of the government property and in case of attack will make the best fight in my power but cannot disguise my apprehensions that the danger is very great. The swamps of the Great and Little Pee Dee (rivers) would afford an impenetrable shelter for hundreds of men and I have been told that several prisoners have already escaped." [63]

Another message on September 17 to Naval Constructor Murray at the Mars Bluff Naval Yard gives further proof of the

[62] Op. cit., Means, 1
[63] Ibid, Means, 2

Commandant's concern for the safety of the Naval Yard and the surrounding installations.

"You will order all of the workmen at the Yard with the exception of the six married men to remain there tonight. Turn them over to Mr. McLenaghan (Acting Commissary for the Naval Yard) and direct him to post a guard at the Rail Road Bridge for the purpose of arresting Yankee prisoners. Also tell him to station a party of five men at the Mars Bluff Ferry for the same object."[64]

Another message was telegraphed to General J. W. Trapier, Commander of the Fourth Military District of South Carolina, headquartered in Georgetown, S.C. In this message Means stated that a large number of prisoners had escaped from the P.O.W. camp at Florence and were attempting to make their way to the coast. Lt. Means went on to state that one of these escapees had been captured at the railroad bridge near the Naval Yard and that three score had managed to cross the Great Pee Dee River and elude their pursuers. Means had placed a guard at the railroad bridge and the ferry. The Lieutenant hoped that General Trapier's forces would be able to interdict the escaped Yankee prisoners before they could reach the coast where they could contact one of the Yankee blockading ships and escape, carrying news of the Confederate Naval effort at Mars Bluff.

The requests for added security from the commander of the Marion Courthouse Naval Station gained the attention of his commanders. Apparently the naval high command planned to assign a Marine Guard to the *CSS Peedee*. In late 1864, 2nd Lt. Ruffin Thomson, Confederate States Marine Corps, wrote home "that he understood that he would probably be ordered to the *CSS Peedee*." [65]

These occurrences were proven by some of the landsite work that our team accomplished along the gas pipeline right of way near the

---

[64] Op. cit., Means, 3

[65] Ralph W. Donnelly, The Confederate States Marine Corps: The Rebel Leathernecks, (White Mane Publishing Co., Shippensburg, PA) 265

site of the old naval yard. There is an undulating stretch of ground north east and across the county dirt road from baseline point H with a small bluff that is higher than the surrounding terrain. On the western side of the pipeline that crosses the crest of this bluff while using metal detectors, we discovered a small cache of lead Enfield rifle bullets in .577 caliber. These appear to have been drawn from rifles using a worm and a ramrod instead of having been fired. It is very possible that this area was the point that Mean's camp guards unloaded their rifles after returning from guard duty.

Lt. Edward Means, CSN, had no idea that Rear-Admiral Dahlgren, USN, commanding the South Atlantic Blockading Squadron, was utilizing similar information in attempting to interest his high command in an assault similar to the Lieutenant's worst nightmare. Admiral Dahlgren had made mention of two citizens of South Carolina arriving at Hilton Head who had "fled rebeldom to avoid conscription. They report the vessel in the Peedee as a gunboat, but not able to get down yet, want of water."[66] This statement was made on October 26, 1864.

Three days later, on October 29, Dahlgren ordered the steamer *USS Philadelphia* to proceed along with the *USS Canandaigua,* a sloop of war mounting three guns and making 10 knots, to the entrance of Winyah Bay and relieve the *USS Pawnee.* An order was to be delivered to Commander Balch of the *Pawnee* that stated,

"I have been informed that the rebels have built a gunboat on the Pedee, which may be expected to come down as soon as the river is high enough. She is said to be of light draft and to carry eight guns of which two are ten inch. The accounts may be exaggerated, but it is well to be prepared. You will take position in the channel and prevent the vessel from getting out to sea." [67]

[66] Op. cit., *Official Records of the Union and Confederate Navies*, Series 1, Vol. 16, 357
[67] Ibid, Official Records of the Union and Confederate Navies, Series 1, Vol. 16, 357

A few days later on November 2, 1864, from aboard his flagship the *USS Harvest Moon*, Dahlgren sent this confidential message to the United States Secretary of the Navy Gideon Welles in Washington, D.C.

"Sir: This will be handed to the Department by Mr. Ward, who has very recently fled from his home in South Carolina. He represents to me that he lived at Kingstree, (Williamsburg County), on the Northeastern Railroad, leading north from Charleston and has always been a Union man and has now abandoned house and property rather than serve in the Rebel Army, which was about to be forced on him by conscription. He has taken the oath of allegiance and his acquaintance with the country where he resided may be turned to good account if the government is disposed to the undertaking."

Dahlgren continues his message stating that Mr. Ward claims that the Confederate armies derive supplies from his neighborhood. Dahlgren goes on to suggest a military operation of cutting the Northeastern Railroad by boat crews that could be dispatched up the Santee River. These boat crews or a landing party coupled with a small troop of cavalry could ascend the Great Pee Dee River in mixed force and attack the Wilmington, Columbia, and Augusta Railroad leading to Wilmington at Mars Bluff, South Carolina. He expresses the belief that if these movements develop rapidly, they would permit occupation between the two rivers and could serve as a base for further operations. Once Georgetown was taken, then the Great Pee Dee River could be entered and an armed reconnaissance made to destroy the gunboat building at Mars Bluff and an attempt made to free the Union prisoners at Florence. Dahlgren stresses the need for secrecy and claims that the season is propitious for prompt action. [68]

---

[68] Op. cit., *Official Records of the Union and Confederate Navies*, Series 1, Vol. 16, 39-40

Furthermore, while all of concerns about escaped prisoners of war and the threat of invasion and destruction of the Naval Yard, the Confederate high command had to contend with Union General William T. Sherman's invasion of Georgia and his army's impending attack on the people of South Carolina. Things were getting a bit out of hand for the Confederacy and the future looked doubtful. The new nation's currency had plummeted due to the successful efforts of counterfeiting of the currency by the United States government as a direct clandestine war effort to destroy the economy of the new American nation; the fact that the Confederate dollar was only backed by faith in the strength of the Government and not by gold or silver; and that the nations of Europe were beginning to doubt the ability of the nation to succeed on the battlefield in gaining their independence from the United States.

Lt. Means, being an honourable man, voices his concerns over budgetary matters in several telegrams. One to Secretary Mallory on January 4, 1865 mentions that he is attempting to arrange provisions for the yard's compliment of workers for the coming year and is suffering embarrassment for want of funds.[69]

On the 22nd of February 1865, the Naval Yard paymaster stated to Secretary Mallory that there is over $100,000.00 needed to pay back wages for three months to his workmen, contracts for provisions, for the pay of his officers, and for the past 60 days requisitions that had been delivered. And still there were no funds forthcoming. [70]

Usually on a dig, one expects to find many items of a personal nature. Interestingly, in the almost two decades that the CSS Peedee Research and Recovery Team explored both the land and underwater sections of the Intensive Survey, we only found one coin....and it was post war, an Indian Head penny dated 1875.

[69] Op. cit., Means, 63
[70] Ibid, Means, 72

That coin turned up on the old wagon road in the swamp between the ferry site and roadbed of the railroad spur line into the Naval Yard. Of course, the Confederate States of America never minted any coins for circulation using only paper money instead. But normally, when excavating other occupied Civil War sites, we have recovered large United States pennies and other coinage minted by foreign countries such as England, Spain, Austria, and France that were being used as tender by the Confederate soldiers. This time though, and on this site, we did not find any period coinage. This failure to recover even a sample of period coinage during our intensive surveys may give a hint to the austerity of the workmen at the Mars Bluff Naval Yard. ❧

Chapter 12

BY THIS TIME, GENERAL Robert E. Lee was embattled by General U. S. Grant and locked into trench warfare at Petersburg, Virginia in an attempt to prevent the Union forces from reaching Richmond. The Confederacy had been severed along the Mississippi River almost two years previously by the collapse of Vicksburg. The western Confederate states and territories were under blockade in the Gulf of Mexico. Sherman was marching through the South and preparing to enter South Carolina. The northern invaders planned to put South Carolina to the torch embittered as they were over the state having been the first to secede.

January 2, 1865, the first elements of General William T. Sherman's Federal army entered South Carolina after resting and resupplying at Savannah, Georgia for over three weeks. By January 15 they had reached Beaufort and were forming a two-prong advance into the state.

Lt. Means, CSN, and his staff began making arrangements for the possible evacuation and protection of government property of the Mars Bluff Naval Yard in mid December. Word had reached the naval yard that two engines for the torpedo boat had arrived at Georgetown aboard the blockade runner *Carolina*. The naval yard commander eagerly encouraged their being shipped up the Great Pee Dee River so that they could be placed aboard the torpedo boats being completed there. This was on December 6, 1864. The naval personnel attached to the *CSS Peedee* expected these two torpedo boats to be powerful auxiliaries to the gunboat.

By the first of January some definitive plans were established. On the 12th of January, 1865, the Lieutenant advised the Secretary of the Confederate Navy that the engines for the torpedo boats had arrived and work on those vessels was advancing. In another communiqué to Secretary Mallory on January 14, 1865, Means stated that the engines for the tender were lost when Union forces captured Port Columbus, Georgia. Means mentions that even with no engines, he plans to go ahead and complete the 150' tender that is under construction to support the *CSS Peedee.* He is of the opinion that if the tender is launched, then much of the valuable machinery from the Mars Bluff Naval Yard could be placed aboard the vessel and towed up river to a place of safety until the Yankee horde passed.[71]

The bombardment of Confederate Ft. Fisher on the peninsula below Wilmington, N.C. began on January 12, 1865 and ended on the 15th. This Union victory allowed General Terry to gain a foothold on North Carolina soil. He would maintain it through the remainder of the war, finally linking up with General Sherman after Sherman's destructive march through South Carolina and the crossing of the Great Pee Dee River at Cheraw, S.C

The *CSS Peedee* is finally complete and battle ready. Her commander and crew only await high water and orders to began their voyage downriver and out to sea. But the national affairs of the Confederate States are in desperate straits. Work continues at the Mars Bluff Naval Yard on the vessels being built. The tender is near completion and afloat, one torpedo boat is launched, and work progresses on a steamer in an attempt to get her into the water in several weeks.

[71] Op. cit., Means, 65

January turns into February and the river is still high. Orders for the *Peedee* have not arrived, but Union forces have marched into the middle of the state and are engaged by Confederate forces in Orangeburg and Aiken on the 11th of February. On the 16th of February, Lt. General William Joseph Hardee commanding Hardee's Corps, Confederate States Army, began the evacuation of Charleston, South Carolina, unable to stem the Yankee tide any longer. His withdrawal would see his troops cross the Great Pee Dee River at Mars Bluff in a few days, a disheartening sight for the forces stationed at the Mars Bluff Naval Yard.

By the 18th of February Columbia, South Carolina was captured and in flames, destroyed by the vengeful Northern invaders.

Meanwhile, back at the Mars Bluff Naval Yard on the Great Pee Dee River, Lt. Means telegraphed Confederate Captain S. S. Lee and advised him that the surrounding countryside was in a terrible state of confusion owing to Sherman's progress through the state and the rumors of the capturing of Columbia and the evacuation of Charleston.[72]

[72] Op. cit., Means, 70

Evidently, two days later the naval forces of the Marion Courthouse Naval Station and the Confederate Naval Yard at Mars Bluff [73] were ordered to retreat to Cheraw. Lt. Morgan had arrived from Charleston with a force of seven men along with ample wagons to load and transport the Navy Yard's munitions to the Cheraw Ordnance Dump approximately 58 miles upriver from Mars Bluff. On the 22 of February, Means dispatched Assistant Paymaster S. Banks to Richmond, Va. on an errand, advising him to report to him at Cheraw, S.C. upon his return. The intent to evacuate the Naval Yard, even though unwritten, is evident in this message.

On the same day the yard commander contacted Secretary Mallory and advised that he had just returned from a consultation with the military authorities in Florence, S.C. He did not get to meet with Lt. General Hardee but instead met with the commander of the Hardee's artillery division, Colonel Hardy. Lt. Means was told by Colonel Hardy that the entire Confederate Army, all 10,000 of them, were moving towards Cheraw and that the area surrounding the Naval Yard would be left some distance from friendly lines. Means continues to state that he is observing orders and will evacuate the Navy Yard and proceed to Cheraw.

His plans are then stated. He and his command will launch the tender on February 23 and place everything of importance belonging to the government on board and move it up river and, if necessary, sink the tender with the equipment on board where it can be raised once the emergency has passed. The torpedo boat will be made ready and moved within four to five days, assisting the moving of the tender up river. This was a secret document and as such was given to Paymaster Banks to deliver to the Secretary in person. Means also states his intention to detach 20 men to protect the buildings where possible. [74] However, being an hon-

---

[73] Op. cit., Means, 73 page back, 74
[74] Ibis, Means, 74-75

ourable man and realizing the indebtedness of the Confederate Naval Department to the population living around the Mars Bluff area, he planned to leave much of the Naval Yard's buildings intact so that the material could be recovered by the populace in return for some of the unpaid debt.

Then, on the same day, in another dispatch to the commanding officer at Florence, he states that he plans to put all of his mechanics back to work in the Army as soon as his detachment reaches Cheraw. There is also mention of his plans to destroy the railroad bridge across the Great Pee Dee River in observance of earlier orders.[75] ک

[75] Op. cit., Means, 76, 79

Chapter 13

IT IS LATE IN the day on February 28, 1865. Previously, Lt. Oscar Johnston had received orders to place the *CSS Peedee* under way and steam up the Great Pee Dee River to Cheraw, 56 miles away, and prepare to cover the flank of Lt. General Hardee's withdrawal of his army from the advancing front of General Sherman's United States Army.

The engineers and the black gang fired up the Confederate Gunboat's boilers and developed a good head of steam. Then, with the command of "All ahead, Full", the vessel's propellers bit into the muddy water of the Great Pee Dee River. With the rudder hardover, the helmsman swung the large warship into mid-channel, pointed her bow up stream, and the first combat mission of the *CSS Peedee* began. The new Confederate warship was finally going in harm's way. Her first mission: To cover the withdrawal of the Confederate Army from Cheraw, South Carolina.

Her crew was excited. The main battle crews stood by the big guns. Passed Midshipman Clayton, commanding the amidships 9" Dahlgren, watched as the riverbanks slid past the vessel as she plunged upstream.

The 7" Brooke Rifle pivot mounted on the bow, was under the command of 2nd Lt. John R. Price, and 1st Lt. David A. Telfair commanded the 6.4" rifle on the stern. Telfair watched as the froth from the ship's propellers dispersed in her wake.[76]

[76] Michael O. Hartley, "The Mars Bluff Navyl Yard, An Archaeological Evaluation", (SCIAA, Columbia, SC) 1983,6.

Meanwhile, gun crew members for the ship's battery charged the 6.4" and 7" Brooke shells in the ship's magazine with fresh gun powder and then plugged each shell's fuse hole with cotton tow to protect their charges from dampness. Passboxes were checked for the correct size fuses for each of the guns, 6.4, 7, and 9 inchers. Then, under stern orders of smoking lamps out, two shells of each caliber were moved from the magazine to the gundeck and placed beside the Dahlgren cannon and the Brooke rifles. Deadly brass percussion fuses were screwed into the snouts of one each of the 6.4" and 7" shells, the safety wires attached and secured, and then the fused shells were placed beside each appropriate gun. The remaining shells were fused in the same manner except that the safety wires were removed from the shells. Meanwhile, each of the Brooke rifles were rammed with the appropriate number of powder bags, 8 pounds of powder for the 6.4, and 12 pounds for the 7" [77], and then the fused shells were cautiously eased down the greased tubes so that their red brass sabots rested against the powder bags that occupied each gun's chamber.

Clayton's 9" smoothbore gun was charged with 13 one pound powder bags and one of the huge round 9" solid shot balls weighing 150 pounds. This gun, useful for battering fortifications, emplacements, and casting broadsides against enemy vessels was a massive instrument of destruction. Clayton viewed the gun with pride. He and his gun crew had practiced daily, as had the members of the two Brooke crews until all of the gun crews served their guns rapidly and with skill.

Six hours later, the men aboard the *CSS Peedee* could hear the muted sounds of musketry and artillery. The battle for Cheraw was underway. As the vessel approached her station near the bridge at Cheraw crossing the Peedee River, a petty officer was dispatched to shore with orders to contact General Hardee's staff and present

[77] Warren Ripley, Artillery Ammunition of the Civil War, (Litton Educational Publishing Inc., New York, NY, 1970) 136

Lt. Johnston's compliments and advise the General that the *CSS Peedee* was on station, guns primed, and awaiting orders.

The town of Cheraw was heavily fortified. Munitions, supplies, governmental records, and private possessions from the evacuation of Charleston and its environs filled the town's warehouses. Confederate ordnance had been placed in a vast ammunition dump near the river. Rifle trenches and gun emplacements bordered the town creating an aura of strong defense. Unfortunately, there was not enough manpower to man the well-designed bastions, so the Confederate army had begun a retreat by the time that the *CSS Peedee* arrived. The petty officer returned to the ship with the orders from the General's staff to stand by and protect the withdrawal and the firing of the bridge across the river to prevent the Yankee invaders from crossing the Great Pee Dee River.

The men of the *CSS Peedee* watched as the rear guard of the Confederate Army withdrew across the Pee Dee River Bridge and lit the powder train that would demolish the structure.

The need to engage the northern army never arrived. When the invaders entered Cheraw, they discovered the bounty stored in the private homes and warehouses, including eight wagonloads of fine Madeira wine that Charleston merchants had sent upriver for safe keeping. A victory party among the officers commenced along with wholesale looting by the Union troops. The Confederate vessel stood by, her crew watchful as the burning bridge collapsed into the Great Pee Dee River and the Yankee invaders looted the town; unable to fire for fear of destroying the town and killing unarmed citizens.

Sherman's Yankee army would have to wait several days for a pontoon bridge to be brought up from the rear and assembled before they could take up the pursuit of the retreating Confederates. By that time, General Hardee would have linked up with General of the Army Joseph Johnston and together they would prevent a stronger barrier against Sherman's forces and stall their uniting with General Terry's Union Army that was advancing from Wilmington, N.C. The *CSS Peedee's* first mission had been a success without firing a shot. Preparations were made to turn the ship about and travel back downstream to the Naval Yard now that the threat had passed.

It could have happened this way. We don't know the details of that voyage. There is no surviving record of the ship's action. We only know that the *CSS Peedee* covered Hardee's withdrawal from Cheraw, South Carolina, and then returned to her home port. However, there is this eye witness report from a Union officer at Cheraw on the evening of March 3, 1865. This officer stated that:

> "There was a Rebel gunboat here last night. A letter taken with mail from one of the gunboat officers says the boat is too large to manoeuvre well in this stream, and speaks of it as 'the remnant of the C.S. Navy'. It is commanded by Capt. Johnston."[78]

No further information has been forthcoming about the only wartime cruise of the *CSS Peedee*. ⟩

---

[78] Thomas Ward Osborn,The Fiery Trail, A Union Officer's Account of Sherman's Last Campaign, (University of Tennessee Press, Knoxville, TN) 163

Chapter 14

THE PEEDEE'S CREW SAFELY turned the large steamer around in the upper narrows of the Great Pee Dee River below Cheraw. They had no idea of what the future held for them. Their government was in flight, they had not been paid for several months, their families were facing destitution, communications between the various departmental army and naval commands were disrupted, and re-supplying for their immediate operations were in doubt. Lt. Johnston ordered that the vessel steam for her homeport downriver at the Mars Bluff Naval Yard. Once there, then the officers of the Naval Yard and the small fleet of vessels moored there could assess the current situation and, perhaps, continue the war to secure the independence of their homeland.

Sometime around March 8, 1865, with no orders arriving from any of the district commanders, Lt. Edward Means summoned his officers to a meeting at the Mars Bluff Naval Yard. Passed Midshipman Clayton stated many years later that Charleston and Wilmington had fallen and Union General Edward Potter's cavalry was raiding within the borders of South Carolina. Clayton continued in his remembrances by saying that "(we) not being able to hear anything from the Navy Department, and the river being too low to let us out to sea, Lt. Oscar Johnston called a council of his officers, and we determined to burn the ship and navy yard and try to reach General Joseph E. Johnston's Confederate army." [79]

[79] Op. cit., Clayton, 106

Lieutenants Means and Johnston were in agreement that there was little contact with any of the higher command. Lt. Means had received orders prior to the *CSS Peedee's* mission to Cheraw to destroy the railroad bridge across the Great Pee Dee River and sever the railroad connections to the state of North Carolina as well as to prepare for the destruction of the naval yard. There is no doubt that he intended to follow these orders. Ensign Sturgis Center's report following the conclusion of hostilities between the two nations confirms this. He states that the *CSS Peedee's* tender, a new ship of 128 feet with a beam of 22 feet lies above the railroad bridge and was filled both on deck and below deck with machinery of all kinds belonging to the Mars Bluff Naval Yard.[80]

Historical facts are not conclusive about the date of destruction of the *CSS Peedee*. Every recorded remembrance seems to indicate that the ship was scuttled on Saturday night, the 18th of March, 1865, at 10:00 P.M. Clayton supports the date stating that he recalled the event between March 15 and March 18, 1865. A more modern account recorded by a reporter for the Charleston News and Courier, July 10, 1938, in that he states that the vessel was destroyed at 10:00 P.M. on Saturday the 18th of March, 1865. It is stated that the explosion of the vessel was witnessed by the remaining officers and crew of the Naval Yard and heard by some of the citizenry as far away as Florence.

While so much of the story of the Mars Bluff Naval Yard and the ships that were built there as well as the late war remembrances of the men involved in that clandestine operation are veiled; our continued research raises some interesting concepts. For instance, one can only help suspecting that since Lt. Charles Hasker was still with the *CSS Peedee* at the time of its demise, and his records indicating that he was the last seaman aboard the ill-fated *CSS Virginia*, and that he applied the quickmatch that scuttled that vessel; then was

[80] Op. cit., Center

his role the same in the destruction of the *Peedee?* After all, he would have had direct knowledge of how to accomplish such a task.

Following the destruction of the Naval Yard and the *CSS Peedee* the personnel from both left the area. Lt. Means went home to Fairfield, South Carolina, as noted in the family sketch presented by his daughter Frances Augusta Means.[81]

Passed Midshipman Clayton and others of the officers and men of the *CSS Peedee* and the Mars Bluff Naval Yard entrained for Sumter, S.C. From there, they marched to Camden, where Clayton and Lt. Price were ordered to carry dispatches to Commodore Hunter, CSN, at Augusta, Georgia. The other members of their unit received orders to report to various commands remaining within the Confederacy. Clayton continued to mention in his remembrances that the state of South Carolina was destroyed by Union General Sherman and that he should be placed with Attila the Hun and King Allaric I, ruler of the Visigoths, in receiving justice.[82]

Admiral Dahlgren stated in a March 28, 1865 report to the United States Secretary of the Navy Gideon Welles that "The State (South Carolina) is completely on its back. The chief danger is from lack of food, the season for planting is at hand, and the freedmen have not generally agreed on terms with the landowners...."

The War of Southern Independence was ending. The last warship of the Confederate States of America, the *CSS Shenandoah*, being the only Confederate vessel to circumnavigate the globe, fired the last cannon shot of the Civil War at a United States whaling ship in the waters off the Aleutian Islands. She then sailed to England and surrendered to the British Admiralty, finally furling the colors of the Confederate States of America on November 6, 1865.

---

[81] Op. cit., Frances Augusta Means
[82] Op. cit., Clayton, 106

CSS Shenandoah hauled out for repairs at Melbourne, Australia

Chapter 15

BOB AND DEBBIE BUTLER journeyed to Baton Rouge, Louisiana on June 8, 1996. Their intention was to study the order book of Lt. Edward Means held in the collection of Louisiana State University's Library. Debbie was allowed to transcribe the order book within a closed room under guard. No one could accompany her, so Bob waited patiently for the two days necessary to copy Lt. Mean's order book in its entirety. At that time the book had not been published. Other researchers that we had interviewed during our search for information on the Mars Bluff Naval Yard had informed us that the book contained nothing more than normal yard requisitions and work details

John Belcner and David Jones in cross trench

After typing the results, the excited duo returned to South Carolina. CSS Peedee Research and Recovery Team members met and studied the transcript that Debbie had made. The order book held a world of information about day to day operations at the Naval Yard. It revealed a tremendous amount about the problems that the commander was experiencing, the citizens of the area surrounding the Confederate operation on the Great Pee Dee River, the war efforts and industrial demands of the Confederate Navy, and supported our theory that the ship had been off-loaded before being destroyed. Lt. Means's reports to his superiors in the last pages of the order book confirmed the plans for leaving a detail to see to the preservation of government property where possible and the protection of the yard's machinery by sinking it in the river so that it could be recovered when the Yankee threat had passed. He detailed the planned destruction of the Naval Yard, the ships that had been built there, and the equipment that would be used in carrying out the orders that he had received from the Department of the Navy.

These pages that Bob and Debbie had rescued from obscurity confirmed our suppositions as to how the naval yard had operated in its last days as well as detailing the necessary search pattern that needed to be employed in the coming months. The contents of Ensign Center's report confirmed what had become of the equipment and the fourteen buildings of the Mars Bluff Naval Yard. Archaeologist Michael Hartley's report of 1983 that SCIAA had given the team gave tremendous insight as to the possible disposition of the remaining undiscovered armament of the *CSS Peedee*. These three valuable repositories of information, after study and comparison, created conclusive history to the unrecorded events of the last days of the Confederate Naval effort at Mars Bluff.

The CSS Peedee Research and Recovery Team's work continued at the site through the summer. Chris Amer and Lynn Harris invited the research team to address the South Carolina Maritime Archaeology Conference scheduled in Charleston for September 28, 1996. Our work and discoveries had been recognized. The team presented an exhibit, spoke at the Maritime Conference, and received the First Place Exhibit Award for the annual conference.

Further historical discoveries at the Mars Bluff Naval Yard site followed in the months ahead. Team members were able to locate the area of the forge and the turpentine distillery that lay within the hilly upper reaches of the Naval Yard. Building sites were plotted by intensive metal detector searches throughout the land area of the Intensive Survey. Wrought iron nails usually marked the outlines and dimensions of former building sites as well as the occasional uncovered pieces of tabby or bricks from pillars and foundations. These all attested to the removal of over half of the fourteen buildings left intact when the personnel vacated the Mars Bluff Naval Yard. These findings indicated the vast landmass that had been utilized during this period of naval endeavor. An area near the fish cleaning shed and extending down the length of the driveway of the Clemmons property was examined. Occupational items found correctly asserted that this area had been the scene of massive logging operations prior to, during, and following the Civil War. The hoped for area of a flooded dry dock turned out to be an excavation site suspected of providing fill for the tram line that passed along the perimeter of the Naval Yard.

Beneath the water, Bob and his divers confirmed that the area suspected of being a logging operation was that indeed. A very old and deep log holding pond lay just north of the Clemmons boat ramp. Scores of cut logs varying in lengths of fourteen to fifteen feet, all felled by hand with axes, had sunk and filled the vast pond. Several of these were removed and examined. Eleven of the examined logs measured the same lengths and the tapered cuts of axmen illustrated the method of logging used at the time.

In 2006, the CSS Peedee Research and Recovery Team agreed to a continuation of the original Intensive Survey at the request of SCIAA. The idea presented was to extend the boundaries further downriver to take in several hundred yards below the highway bridge. The team began to run short surveys, both by diver examination and by underwater metal detection beneath and below the twin bridges across the Peedee and into the new area. This was a treacherous area for divers due to the continued collection of flotsam and debris around the bridge supports. The channel narrowed in that area due to the obstructions presented by the held logs and downed trees. The current increased in speed and the divers were limited in what could be performed at that point.

Bob Butler, Ted Gragg andRonnie Sommersett

We also began to pay more attention to the opposite shore and the area fronting it, even though we knew that the dragline operations of the salvage crew in 1954 probably had scattered any artifact fields that were in that area. Still, we included that section of water into our searches. Meanwhile we continued to work the original land and water site as well.

One day in the late fall of 2005 three of us, Chad, Bob, and I, decided that the river area was too cold and uncomfortable to work in the water. Instead we investigated a portion of the old tram line that lay above and to the southern corner of the Clemmons property. We encountered a massive reading on our metal detectors between the roots of two very large trees. The three of us began digging. We dug and then dug some more. It was hard work digging between the massive roots of the trees but success followed.

We were able to move enough earth from between the trees to enable us to see what our machines had indicated lay there. The needles of the metal detectors had pegged, indicating a very large metallic object. What could it be? The missing ordnance magazine for the Naval Yard, perhaps. No such luck though. The hidden object was huge. We couldn't move it as it was just too big! We were forced to excavate around it as it lay buried beneath the roots of the trees. Finally enough earth had been moved so that we could view the artifact.

Vigorously brushing the dirt away from the artifact as we revealed a set of huge coiled springs attached to a support holding two massive train car wheels. We had located a broken supporting section of a railroad car truck from the early twentieth century. It had probably lain there undisturbed since the 1920s or so, tossed there by a yard crew working on the nearby railroad. Still, the excitement had been intense. While the find had no bearing on the yard, it had still presented a challenge and some labor intensive fun.

Later that year our land team investigated the stone supports of the power station for the yard again while the underwater unit continued the grid by grid search for artifacts. Again, each item located was recorded, tagged, and preserved. Opportunities continued to arise that afforded us a glimpse into the past from the analyses of the recovered artifacts. Mr. Richard Johnson of Historical Iron Works in Conway, South Carolina, offered to conduct an analyses on some samples of the cleats or eye hooks and cannister that had been recovered from the underwater site of the Mars Bluff Naval Yard.

His report is as follows:

Cannister (40mm shot)

Pig iron and a small amount of manganese were melted in a sintering furnace and poured into a sand mold. The tough casting probably resembled several balls on a long rod. They were simply broken up and stored until they could be shipped to a munitions factory. The sample I received was in good condition. It was cut in half and the face was polished to a 600 grit finish. It was then etched for 6 hours in a 10% solution of Muratic acid and water. The shot ball is very hard, slightly malleable, but will chip under force. It is of 1860 type production.

The Eye Hook

This hook is similar to many found at the Mars Bluff Naval Yard site and is made of true wrought iron. The sample I received would be cut the entire length and polished. The hook was etched in the same acid solution as before for 12 hours to reveal the grain structure. Where the siliceous slag (iron silicate) was, now is a void. This alloy is typical of what the first and simplest iron furnaces (called Bloomerys) that could produce directly from ore. The ore was heated with charcoal in a small furnace, usually made of stone and blown upon with a bellows. Most of the impurities were burned out leaving a spongy mass of iron mixed with slag. The sponge ball was hammered until the slag was evenly distributed. Our sample saw very little hammering; it is also soft metal that can be easily cut with a knife (typical of early charcoal iron). The alloy is of extremely poor quality and, although good for the time, my guess is that the iron in this hook was produced locally around 1820-1860.

Visual analyses such as this on recovered items aided us greatly in our research of the layout of the Mars Bluff Naval Yard, the placement of items on and in the various vessels built there, and the manner of construction of the various recovered artifacts. This information aided further in understanding the everyday working skills of the yard craftsmen and laborers as well as the location of possible light manufacturing operations within the naval yard complex.

All of the understanding of the physical work centers of the archaeological site aided us in the underwater search for both small and large artifacts. And of course, in September of 2006, we located the 6.4 Brooke Rifle. Metallic anomalies observed within the search area suggested by the possible deck arrangement of the two located guns indicated the presence of the third cannon.

The CSS Peedee Research and Recovery Team approached SCIAA concerning the next phase of the operation at this time and requested consideration for a salvage permit to work on raising the cannon that we had located during the intensive survey. Unknown to us at the time, other events were beginning to unfold that would change the way that the attempt to recover the two cannon would be made.

Sadly, Wiles Clemmons, an early member of the Peedee Research and Recovery Team, died shortly after selling his property fronting the river.

A group of legislators from Florence proposed a bill in the State House that would set the Great Pee Dee River area above and below the railroad bridge off limits for any future recovery of artifacts as a means to protect the history of the area. This bill was presented in both the South Carolina House and the Senate. When the bill came up for vote it passed and was forwarded to the Governor of South Carolina.

A representative from the Governor's office contacted me and asked if our team would be in agreement with the passage of the law. Bob and I conferred and agreed that during the present course of events this would be the best way to protect the valuable history and artifacts hidden beneath the waters of the Great Pee Dee River. I returned the call to the Governor's aide and expressed our hearty agreement with the proposed law. The Governor's signature would protect a very sensitive archaeoligical site.

A year passed. A grant to salvage the cannons of the *CSS Peedee* was given to the University of South Carolina, South Carolina Institute of Anthropology and Archaeology Department by the Drs. Bruce and Lee Foundation of Florence, S.C. SCIAA, once funded, began work anew to accomplish this mission under the leadership of Chris Amer. East Carolina University of North Carolina fielded a Summer Field school under the guidance of Dr. Lynn Harris in May of 2009. Bob Butler and I were asked to assist in the location of the guns of the *CSS Peedee* along with providing charts and baseline information to the SCIAA teams. Assistance in this project came from throughout the surrounding region and illustrated the intense interest in preserving the history of the Confederate naval effort on the Great Pee Dee River. Local scuba dealers, property owners on both the Florence and Marion banks of the river rendered assistance to the research groups, the South Carolina Civil War Museum opened its archives and exhibits to the student researchers, and community volunteers manned shovels and sifters during the land excavations. This past summer of 2010, underwater filming of both of the partially exposed cannon was accomplished. Interestingly, the markings on the exposed trunnion of the Dahlgren gun match those traced on the trunnion and recorded by the dive team of the CSS Peedee Research and Recovery Team on June 28, 1996.

The future looks very bright for the continued research of the *CSS Peedee*. Efforts are underway to raise the 9" Dahlgren and the 6.4" Brooke within the next few years. Observations of the possible wreck site of the *CSS Peedee* have been made electronically and verified. The whereabouts of the remains of the wreck are known now. After years of mishandling the wreck and its hidden treasures are protected by the laws of South Carolina. Meanwhile, the artifacts from the Mars Bluff Naval Yard as well as the sampled artifacts of the supplies and ordnance thrown overboard from the *CSS Peedee* in preparation for her scuttling while she was moored dockside at the Naval Yard are preserved. These historical artifacts that were recovered by the CSS Peedee Research and Recovery Team are on display at the South Carolina Civil War Museum in Myrtle Beach, South Carolina. ❧

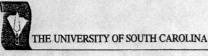

THE UNIVERSITY OF SOUTH CAROLINA

SOUTH CAROLINA INSTITUTE OF ARCHAEOLOGY AND ANTHROPOLOGY

May 23 '95

Received from CSS Pee Dee Recovery Team
two 1½ grape shot, 2 sail rings (thimble?)
and 1 four inch connector tapers a donation
to the South Carolina Institute of Archaeology
and Anthropology.

With thanks.

Christopher F. Amer.
Deputy State Archaeologist for Underwater.

Lynn Harris
SDAMP Manager.

Ted L. Bragg
CSS Pee Dee Recovery Team

1321 Pendleton Street • Columbia, S.C. 29208-0071 • (803) 777-8170 • 734-0567 • 799-1963 • FAX 254-1338

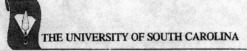

THE UNIVERSITY OF SOUTH CAROLINA

SOUTH CAROLINA INSTITUTE OF ARCHAEOLOGY AND ANTHROPOLOGY

Public Hearing
Wednesday, April 3, 1996
Horry County Museum

A public meeting will be held on Wednesday, April 3, at
11am at the Horry County Museum to process an Intensive
Survey License application for underwater investigations
at Mars Bluff Naval Yard on the Pee Dee River. The license
applicants, the *CSS Pee Dee* Research and Recovery Team,
will present their application to the South Carolina
Institute of Archaeology and Anthropology, other agencies
and the public. Questions, comments and responses will
be heard from these groups. For additional information
about the hearing or the application contact Christopher
Amer at (803)777-8170.

1321 Pendleton Street • Columbia, S.C. 29208-0071 • (803) 777-8170 • 734-0567 • 799-1963 • FAX 254-1338

University of South Carolina

SOUTH CAROLINA INSTITUTE
OF ARCHAEOLOGY AND ANTHROPOLOGY

Certifies That

Ted Gragg

attended a Field Training Course under the supervision of the Underwater
Archaeology Division's Sport Diver Archaeology Management Program in

May, 1996

and is eligible to participate in Maritime Archaeology Field Training projects.

Dr. Bruce E. Rippeteau
Director and State Archaeologist

Lynn Harris, Archaeologist
Sport Diver Archaeology Management Program

Christopher F. Amer
Deputy State Archaeologist For Underwater

S.C.I.A.A.
U.S.C.

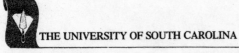

THE UNIVERSITY OF SOUTH CAROLINA

SOUTH CAROLINA INSTITUTE OF ARCHAEOLOGY AND ANTHROPOLOGY

September 3, 1996

Dear Tedd,

We are looking forward to hearing you give a talk at the SC Maritime Archaeology Conference in Charleston on Saturday, September 28. Enclosed is the program for the conference and a map giving directions to the SC Department of Natural Resources on James Island. As a speaker you are not required to pay the registration fee, but will need to pay the $10 for the oyster roast/shrimp broil dinner in the evening. Please let us know by September 20 if you plan to join us for this event so that we have some idea of numbers for catering purposes.

We will be publishing a proceedings of the conference and would like all speakers to bring along a written version of their talk with any photographs or drawings that will be accompany the text. We also need a brief summary of your talk (an abstract) by September 23. If you plan to set up an exhibit or book table, please let us know too.

If you need any further information on the Conference or names and numbers of motels and accomodations in the Charleston area, please contact me.

Sincerely,

Lynn Harris
SCIAA Underwater Archaeology Division, P.O. Box 12448, Charleston SC 29422
Phone: (803)762-6105 Fax: (803)762-5831 E-Mail: harrisl@cofc.edu

SCHEDULE OF EVENTS

9:00-9:30   South Carolina Archaeology
              Week Opening Address: Dr Bruce Rippeteau

              Opening Remarks: Nena Rice
              Conference Chair: Lynn Harris

Avocational Archaeology Research - Chair, Carl Naylor

9:30-10:20   A Submerged Prehistoric Site in the V
              Branch, Cooper River: Doug Boehme

South Carolina Maritime Archaeology Conference

South Carolina Institute Archaeology and Anthropology
University of South Carolina

10:20-11:00   The Mars Bluff Naval Shipyard, Pee I
              River: Tedd Gragg and Bob Butler

11:00-11:20   The History and Underwater Compon
              Limerick Plantation, East Branch, Co
              River: Michelle Mantooth

11:20-12:00   The Aucilla River Prehistory Project i
              Gifford

MARINE RESOURCES CENTER
217 Fort Johnson Rd
September 28, 1996

12:00-1:00   **LUNCHBREAK**

Special Presentations on S.C Maritime History - Chair, Chris Amer

1:00-1:25   Tidecraft of the Southeastern US: Rusty Fleetwood

1:25-1:30   Comic Relief from Archaeology -"Shipworms !": Lou Edens

1:30-2:05   Blockade Runners - A focus on the Charleston
              area: Steven Wise

2:05-2:30   An Update on the *H.L. Hunley* Project:
              Christopher Amer and Gunter Weber

Certificate of Appreciation

Presented to

Pee Dee Research and Recovery Team

Best Exhibit at SC Maritime Archaeology Conference

The South Carolina Institute of Archaeology and Anthropology at the University of South Carolina hereby expresses its appreciation and recognition for service rendered to South Carolina Archaeology and to the People of the State of South Carolina.

Bruce E. Rippeteau
Director and State Archaeologist

28 Sept 1996
on this date

CSS Pee Dee Research and Recovery Group awarded the best exhibit at the conference. L to R: Bob Butler Debbie Coates, Connie Gragg and Ted Gragg

CERTIFICATE OF REGISTRATION

This Certificate issued under the seal of the Copyright Office in accordance with title 17, United States Code, attests that registration has been made for the work identified below. The information on this certificate has been made a part of the Copyright Office records.

Marybeth Peters

REGISTER OF COPYRIGHTS
United States of America

FORM TX
For a Literary Work
UNITED STATES COPYRIGHT OFFICE

TXu 812-851

EFFECTIVE DATE OF REGISTRATION

Month	Day	Year
7	25	9?

DO NOT WRITE ABOVE THIS LINE. IF YOU NEED MORE SPACE, USE A SEPARATE CONTINUATION SHEET.

TITLE OF THIS WORK ▼ C.S.S. PEE DEE RESEARCH & RECOVERY TEAM
THE MARS BLUFF CONFEDERATE NAVAL DEPARTMENT SHIPYARD
INTENSIVE SURVEY REPORT: PHASE I

Bibliography

Babits, Lawrence E., Harris, Lynn, Caudell, Nolen, and Edmonds, Adam. <u>Prehistoric Pottery, Munitions and Caulking Tools: Archaeological and Historical Investigations at Mars Bluff Confederate Shipyard (38 Ma22-91) on The Great Pee Dee River, Program in Maritime Studies History Department</u>, Summer Field School 2009, East Carolina University, 2010, Greenville, N.C.

Babits, Lawrence E., Confederate Artillery Material from the Peedee River, South Carolina. <u>Military Collector and Historian, Journal of the Company of Military Historians</u>, Vol.63, No.1.

Black, Robert C. III. <u>The Railroads of the Confederacy</u>, University of N.C. Press, Chapel Hill, N.C., 1998

Cauthen, Charles E., editor. <u>Journals of the South Carolina Executive Councils of 1861 and 1862</u>, South Carolina Archives Dept., Columbia, S.C., 1956

Center, USN Acting Ensign Sturgis. Report to Lt. Commander R.L. Law, Port Royal, South Carolina, USN., 10-20-1865

Clayton, W.F., <u>A Narrative of the Confederates States Navy</u>. Bulletin Pee Dee Historical Association, 1910. Coker, PC Charleston's Maritime Heritage, 1670-1865

Clayton, W.F., <u>The Confederate States Navy</u>, Harrel's Printing House, Weldon, NC, 1910

Confederate Navy Department Payroll Records, Marion Courthouse Naval Station, Marion, South Carolina, War Department Collection of Confederate Records, section 109.12, Record Group 109, 1825-1900 (bulk 1861-65)

Daniel, Larry J., & Gunter, Riley W,. <u>Confederate Cannon Foundries</u>, Pioneer Press, Union City, Tenn., 1977

Donnelly, Ralph W., <u>Confederate States Marine Corps: The Rebel Leathernecks</u>,White Mane Publishing Co., Shippensburg, PA. 1990

Gragg, Connie B. & Ted L. Gragg, <u>Grid Maps of Mars Bluff Naval Yard</u>, Intensive Survey, 1996, South Carolina, Civil War Museum, SCIAA

Hartley, Michael O., <u>Recovery of the Gunboat Peedee</u>, 1954 SCIAA

Hartley, Michael O., <u>The Mars Bluff Navy Yard, An Archaeological Evaluation</u>, 1983, SCIAA

Hasker, Charles Hazelwood., Boatswain Charles H. Hasker's Recollections. <u>A Graphic Description of the Ironclad and Its Participation in the Memorable Battles - His Autobiographical Note and Lecture Script</u>, Hasker family collection copies, South Carolina Civil War Museum, Myrtle Beach, SC

Marion County Deed Book Z, 1863: 417-418, Marion County, South Carolina

May 1863 letter from Lt. Van R. Morgan to Lt. Commander Jones, Library of Congress Area 8 file, 838-841

Means, CSN Lt. Edward. <u>Order Book 1864</u>, LSU Library Collection, Baton Rouge, LA

Means, Frances Augusta. <u>Family Sketch of Edward Means</u>, Frances Augusta Means, his daughter, Means Letters, University of South Carolina Library, Columbia, SC

Naval History Division, Naval Historical Center, <u>Civil War Naval Chronology 1861-1865</u>, IV47, Washington, D.C., US Government Printing Office

Naval War Records Office. Official Records of the Union and Confederate Navies in the War of the Rebellion, United States, Series I, Vols. 1-27, Series II, vols. 1-3, Government Printing Office, Washington, D.C. 1894-1922

Orvin, Maxwell Clayton, <u>In South Carolina Waters 1861-1865</u>, Nelson's Southern Printing and Publishing Co., Charleston, SC

Osborn, Thomas Ward, <u>The Fiery Trail, A Union Officer's Account of Sherman's Last Campaign</u>, University of Tennessee Press, Knoxville, TN 1986

Ripley, Warren, <u>Artillery and Ammunition of the Civil War</u>, Litton Educational Publishing, Inc., New York, N.Y., 1970

Rogers, James, <u>The Florence Morning News</u>, Article, December 30, 1950

Stanley, William B., "Confederate Ship Never Got To Sea", <u>Charleston News and Courier</u>, July 10, 1938

Still, William N. Jr., <u>Confederate Shipbuilding</u>, University of Georgia Press, Athens, Ga. 1967.

"Raising of the PeeDee", <u>The Columbia Record</u>, November 1, 1954,

Townsend, Leah. "The Confederate Gunboat Pedee", <u>The South Carolina Historical Magazine</u> , Vol. LX, No. 2, April 1959, S.C. Historical Society, Charleston, S.C.

PHOTOGRAPHY: Artifact photography by Charles Hill

About The Author

Ted Gragg

Ted L. Gragg's childhood excursions from his grandparent's summer home at Fort Fisher, N.C., led to a life-long interest in the American Civil War. This interest along with weekend hobbyist searches for American Civil War sites in the South Carolina low country led to his quest for the Confederate Naval Vessel CSS Peedee. After locating the Mars Bluff Naval Yard site on the banks of the Great Pee Dee River in Marion County, South Carolina, he formed the CSS Peedee Research and Recovery Team under the guidance of the South Carolina Institute of Archaeology and Anthropology (SCIAA). These efforts resulted in the recovery and charting of artifacts from the Mars Bluff Naval Yard and the warships built there. Ted and his wife Connie established the South Carolina Civil War Museum in Myrtle Beach, South Carolina, to house the recovered and preserved artifacts.

He and his wife Connie have shared many adventures through their 43 years together. They and their daughters Holly Sasser, Wendy Belcner, son-in-law Maj. John Belcner, and their grandchildren Shelley, Eddie, and Vaughn, enjoy the South Carolina shores and wilderness in continued historical expeditions. ⟩

Feel free to e-mail Mr. Gragg at: lemgragg@gmail.com

CPSIA information can be obtained at www.ICGtesting.com
Printed in the USA
LVOW111058170212

269113LV00002B/3/P